The Murray Rive

Amanda Burdon  Bill Bachman

Front Cover: Tranquil times – majestic river red gums fringe a broad swathe of the Murray at the mouth of Banrock Creek, Banrock station, near Kingston-on-Murray in the South Australian Riverland.

Back Cover: Grand dame of the Murray, historic paddle-steamer *Adelaide*, puffs around Hairpin Bend, downstream of Echuca.

Title page: A black swan dries its wings on a wetland laced with azolla near Barham, 80 km north-west of Echuca.

This spread: Meandering sensually, the Murray (left) emerges from the Snowy Mountains foothills at Towong, in northern Victoria. Weathered snowgums (below) encroach on Davies Plain Track in the Alpine National Park, not far from the Murray River's lofty cradle.

Following spread: Tendrils of mist (main picture) curl among river red gums along Chalka Creek, in Hattah-Kulkyne National Park, north-western Victoria. A male emu (top left) devotedly tends his clutch of eggs in the park. Skippy (bottom left), the inquisitive caretaker of Loxton Historical Village, in north-eastern SA, checks out the camera.

First published in 2000 by Australian Geographic Pty Ltd
PO Box 321, Terrey Hills NSW 2084, Australia
Phone: (02) 9450 2344; Fax: (02) 9450 2990
email: books@ausgeo.com.au

Managing Director: Paul Gregory
Publisher: Howard Whelan
Production/Creative Director: Tony Gordon
Managing Editor, Books: Averil Moffat

Editor: Peter Meredith
Design and Photographic Edit: Moyna Smeaton, Concept Press
Director of Cartography: Will Pringle
Production Managers: Michelle Hessing, Jožica Črnčec
Commissioning Editor: Ian Connellan
Staff Editor: David Scott-Macnab
Picture Research: Chrissie Goldrick
Cartographers: Vicki Gow, James Austin
Proofreading: Frank Povah
Editorial Assistants: Sandy Richardson, Gillian Manning

Photography by Bill Bachman unless otherwise credited

National Library of Australia Cataloguing-in-Publication Data:

Burdon, Amanda.
  The Australian Geographic Book of the Murray River.

  Includes index.
  ISBN 1 86276 028 4.

  Murray River Region (NSW–S. Aust.) – History.
  2. Murray River Region (NSW–S. Aust.) – Description and travel.
  3. Murray River Region (NSW–S. Aust.) – Discovery and exploration.
  4. Murray River Region (NSW–S. Aust.) – Guidebooks.
  I. Bachman, Bill. II. Australian Geographic Pty Ltd. III. Title.

919.4404

⫿ This spread: River red gums in a state of artistic undress (above) at Katarapko Creek, within the Murray River National Park, near Berri in South Australia. Trout-fishing guide Ron Vise and his son Danny paddle out (right) in the hope of a strike near their home at Towong, on the serene upper Murray.

⫿ Contents spread: A misty mid-winter day dawns on the Murray near Tocumwal, in southern NSW.

CONTENTS

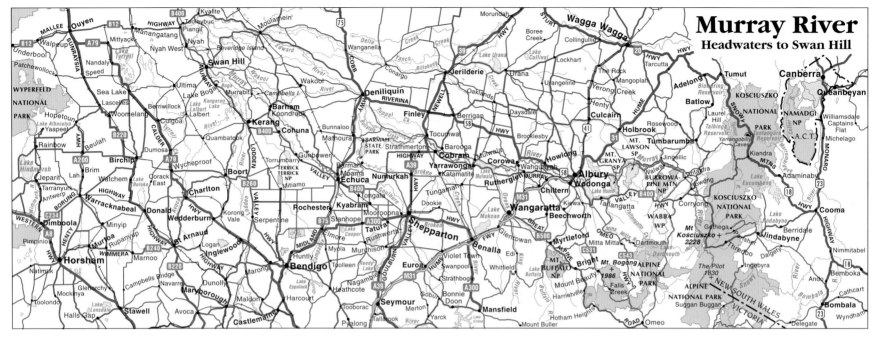

Murray River
Headwaters to Swan Hill

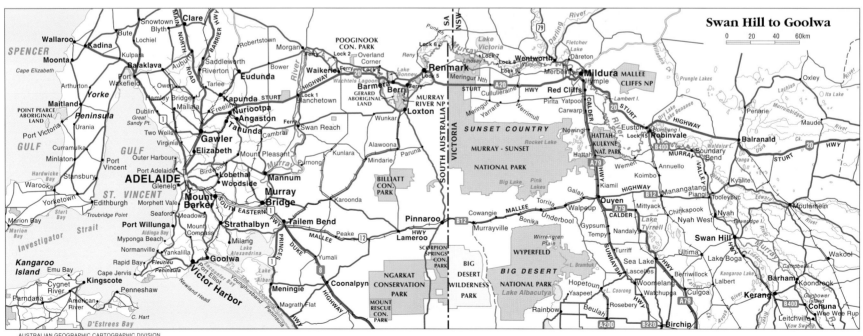

Swan Hill to Goolwa

0   20   40   60km

AUSTRALIAN GEOGRAPHIC CARTOGRAPHIC DIVISION

Foreword

One of the world's magical places is on the red sand dunes atop the limestone cliffs at Bunyip Reach in South Australia. Above, an intense blue sky. Below, an ochre river flowing unbounded by space and time. All around, a forest of grey-green eucalypts reaching to the horizon, and a silence broken only by the calls of corellas and galahs. There is scarcely a sign of humanity.

Who could not be captivated by the romance of a great river like the Murray? It is true that some of the world's rivers are longer, and some may carry more water in a day than does the Murray in a year. But the Murray's claim to greatness is secure because it is a common stream through the lives of many people. It was a lifeline for Aboriginal people for many thousands of years, and no less important to our colonial forebears. Today, it supplies water to many towns and cities and underwrites much of the nation's farm production. The river binds us through its influence on our history, geography and commerce, and through our fascination with the sheer wonder of it all.

To an ecologist like myself, the Murray's hallmark is its changeability. In the days before dams and weirs the river would sometimes contract to salty pools. In the drought of 1914, the junction of the Murray and the Darling was as dry and dusty

as the junction of two country roads, but three years later the river rose in one of the greatest recorded floods. The Murray's flora and fauna evolved to meet those changeable conditions, and they are bonded to them. In the modern, regulated river many of those species find themselves in a more stable environment that favours exotic species like carp and willows. Regulation has also weakened the vital link between the river and its floodplain – both parts of the one ecosystem – and not surprisingly the effects have been profound.

The old river now faces its greatest challenge. Would it matter if the fabled Murray cod and other native species were to disappear? One can visit many rivers around the world and see dams and weirs, carp and willows, but there is only one where you can hope to see a Murray cod. The ecological reality is that we are now taking far too much water from the river, and if it is to retain any of its natural characteristics we will need to make concessions. As the environment continues to change, and the pace of change quickens, we have little time to reconsider.

A first encounter with a great river often inspires a continuing, lifelong exploration. In this book, Amanda Burdon tells of her exploration of the Murray in eloquent words that surely will inspire others. I am certain that you will enjoy her story, together with Bill Bachman's photographic panorama, as it unfolds before you.

Keith Walker,
Environmental Biologist,
The University of Adelaide

Introduction

> I do not know much about gods; but I think that the river Is a strong brown god – sullen, untamed, intractable ...
>
> T.S. Eliot, *Four Quartets*

The Ngarrindjeri people of South Australia believe the giant cod Ponde created the Murray River. Pursued by their spirit ancestor Ngurunderi, the fish thrashed across the landscape, carving oxbows and billabongs with each desperate swish of its powerful tail. Every cod now carries an imprint not only of Ponde's struggle but also of its own travels, the river folk say: on the inner body wall, near the stomach, is a tracery that according to legend is the tree under which the fish was spawned.

The Murray River is awash with stories and secrets as it flows 2520 kilometres from its mountain cradle to the Southern Ocean. When I began my own journey along it, I wanted to hear every one, to soak up the essence of Australia's greatest river. I did my best, but

after months of research I had to concede that no-one can profess to know the Murray intimately. Capricious by nature, it is both promising and uncompromising; restrained by human hand, it is capable of escape acts worthy of Houdini; serene on the surface, it is littered with hidden hazards. And it changes with every season.

The Aboriginals understood its moods best; the way it veiled itself in mist in winter, spilled lazily across the land during spring and summer floods and sulked in pools during dry spells. They knew that the lives of the Murray valley's plants and animals were inextricably linked with the fortunes of the river, and they respected this delicate balance.

The Murray's occupation by European settlers, from the first tentative excursions across the Great Dividing Range to today's complex river regulation, is of a very different nature. Belief in a mythical inland sea first inspired explorers Hamilton Hume and William Hovell, then urged Charles Sturt down the river in a whaleboat in 1829–30. Within a few decades, 863,300 sq. km of land were settled in Queensland, New South Wales, Victoria and SA, the pioneers having followed the river's tributaries upstream. As writer Russell Braddon noted in *River Journeys*, "the mood of the Murray became a sure barometer of the prosperity of each. If she flooded excessively, or dried up vindictively – and she did both with great regularity – economic disasters followed. When she was benign, flocks prospered, harvests flourished, paddle-steamers by the hundred threshed 1000 miles upstream and 1000 miles back ..."

The Murray remains the same maker and breaker of dreams today. To thousands of inland Australians, it is indeed T.S. Eliot's brown god, playing an integral part in Australian society and

▦ Fly fisherman Tom Gleisner (above) checks his line before casting into the placid upper Murray near Towong.

▦ The pea-green waters of the Lindsay River (opposite), an anabranch of the Murray, are fringed by gnarled red gums in Murray Sunset National Park, west of Mildura.

economics. With its major tributaries – the Darling, Murrumbidgee and Goulburn rivers – the Murray drains one-seventh of the Australian landmass. The Murray-Darling Basin supports 40 per cent of the nation's agricultural production (amounting to $10 billion annually) quenches the thirst of more than a million South Australians and helps to generate electricity for NSW, Victoria and the Australian Capital Territory.

▥ The PS *Melbourne* passes through Lock 11 at Mildura (above), one of 13 built along the Murray to aid navigation.

▥ Day is done on the river at Mallee Cliffs State Forest (opposite), near Colignan in north-western Victoria.

The demands made on the Murray River today are immense and often competing. Salinisation, erosion, environmental decline and land degradation have been some of the unfortunate results of human intervention. They are challenges we are only now beginning to face.

Nevertheless, the river I came to know during my travels remains majestic and a much-loved source of incredible abundance and energy. Big cod still cruise its deeper reaches; the spirit of long-gone swagmen, squatters and steamboat captains lingers in the colourful river towns; and the grand old river continues to be a destination for adventure-seekers, as well as a sanctuary for those bent on quiet reflection.

Some of my most enduring memories of the Murray are of fleeting events: of naked boys leaping from red gums into the fast-flowing stream; of the water's velvet lustre at dusk; of a veteran fisherman's easy smile; of an old paddleboat's shrill whistle on an afternoon cruise. This book records my richly rewarding travels along the Murray over several months and seasons in 1998–99 with photographer Bill Bachman, mostly in his Landcruiser, affectionately dubbed Murray. Like our own adventure, it is a rambling river tale punctuated by serendipitous encounters and discoveries. The wonderful thing about the Murray is that it offers both in abundance. Many more surprises await those who follow in our footsteps.

A TORTUOUS PATH

The rays of the setting sun fell across a jigsaw puzzle of stubbled paddocks, lush pastures and barren fields near the township of Tocumwal, in southern NSW. From my seat in the cockpit of a glider 900 m above the landscape, the Murray River was a scarf of sapphire silk uncoiling across the Riverina, its folds and curves caressing sandy shoals and clumps of red gums as far as the eye could see. I was captivated by its sensual form.

As I savoured the view, I remembered a conversation I'd had with one of the Murray's most fervent supporters, Associate Professor Keith Walker, a biologist at the University of Adelaide. "The river we see today will not be the river we'll see tomorrow," he said. "It changes constantly. What inspires me most about it is its great age and wild character and its scarred and tortured history – a history of brief respites in an overwhelmingly harsh climate."

After tumbling out of the timbered mountains of the Australian Alps, the Murray flows across some of the driest terrain on one of the world's driest continents. Fed by a catchment covering 1,061,469 sq. km (14 per cent of Australia's surface area), it collects rivers flowing south from Queensland and NSW and north from Victoria in the saucer-like Murray–Darling Basin, which tilts gently downwards to the west. For more than 2000 km of its 2520 km journey the Murray receives little sustenance other than that provided by its headwater catchment and four of its larger 11 tributaries, the Murrumbidgee, Ovens, Goulburn and Darling rivers. Rainfall in its catchment is erratic and its natural flows reflect this uncertainty.

The river beneath me was relatively shrunken, recovering from a busy late-summer irrigation season. Against the sheen of its surface I could make out the white frames of waterbirds and the skeletons of trees that had surrendered to past events. I saw, too, the imprint of that wider Murray, the floodplain interwoven by wetlands, billabongs and ephemeral lakes, some as ancient as the river itself, that waited for the next great inundation. I knew it would surely come, as surely as it had done in the past.

The making of a river system

The evolution of Australia's greatest river system began at least 100 million years ago (mya). Today you'll see little evidence of its complex origins, for much of its history is secreted in sediments deep beneath the riverbed. Only from the air can one trace the loops of some of its

Limestone deposits (opposite) blaze white in the cliff face of the Murray Gorge north-west of Kingston-on-Murray, in south-eastern SA. The scalloped gorge, 100 m deep in places, began forming as far back as 700,000 years ago when Lake Bungunnia, a large freshwater lake that covered the region, drained and the river carved a channel through the old lakebed.

A LAKE IN THE MAKING

Much of the Murray River's complex geological history can be traced to a very slow uplifting of the land and the movement of sea water into and out of the Murray Basin like a massive tide. About 5-3 million years ago (mya), land in the basin slowly rose. The sea water drained, leaving behind ridges of sand (1). A massive earth uplift (2) south of present-day Swan Reach more than 2 mya dammed the waters of the fledgling Murray River, creating Lake Bungunnia (3). Fed by heavy rain, the freshwater lake swelled to cover some 33,000 sq. km and support tortoises, Murray cod and lungfish up to 3 m long. About 700,000 years ago the lake breached the natural dam (4) and, as it emptied, the Murray River gouged out a new channel that included the cavernous Murray Gorge (5). Sea-level fluctuations (6) have since scoured out the gorge's lower reaches and filled it with sediment, some of which remains on today's floodplain.

Coastline of 2 mya
150 m below present sea level

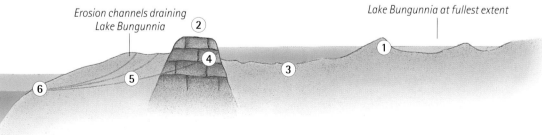

Erosion channels draining
Lake Bungunnia

Lake Bungunnia at fullest extent

ancestral paths – old-timers now choked with clay, sand and gravel that speak of a wetter time, when the rainforested continent was crisscrossed by more plentiful and larger rivers.

The key to the Murray's existence lies in the formation of the Murray–Darling Basin. This had its beginnings in a large, shallow rock depression dating from 350 million years. About 100 mya, as the mountains of the Great Dividing Range began rising through the Earth's surface, a large area of the depression west of the divide began slowly to subside and deepen. Large rivers streaming westward off the emerging highlands filled it with eroded sediments and debris, depositing them layer upon layer, like a multi-decked sandwich.

For most of the past 65 million years, the western portion of the Murray Basin was almost continually covered by warm, shallow seas and marine lakes intruding from the Southern Ocean. These contributed sediments to the basin's floor, including limestone deposits that survive today as crumbling cliffs along the river in South Australia.

After Australia finally separated from the supercontinent Gondwana 50-45 mya, sea levels around the world rose. A finger of salt water, named the Murravian Gulf, extended from the Southern Ocean into the western half of the Murray Basin about 32 mya. At its peak, about 20 mya, it stretched beyond the site of present-day Swan Hill, before retreating around 12 mya.

Vast climate change characterised the next chapter in the basin's history, with the sea repeatedly encroaching and retiring. At every intrusion, the sea spread layers of coarse sand on the basin floor. Over time these became compressed under the gravel and clay

▦ The forested western slopes of the Great Dividing Range are the Murray's cradle. The river, fed by rainwater and snowmelt collected high in the ranges, emerges in the Biggara Valley (above left) in the early stages of its 2520 km course to the Southern Ocean. Along the way, the river nourishes more than 7500 wetlands and numerous ephemeral lakes, including those of the Barmah forest (above), north-east of Echuca.

Like a swathe of sapphire silk, the Murray is draped across the countryside near Whirlpool Corner (above), north of Renmark. . It is one of the slowest-flowing rivers in the world, with an average current speed of just 3 km/h, making it a perfect training ground for rowers (opposite) downstream at Walker Flat, between Mannum and Swan Reach.

deposited by the basin's rivers. At its deepest, the Murray Basin sandwich extended 600 m. The sandy shores of the central Murray favoured by holidaymakers today, and the sand ridges of the mallee region are reminders of the sea's influence.

From 6–4 mya, the westward-flowing rivers chased the retreating sea deep into SA and started forging routes to the Southern Ocean. But just over 3.5 mya their paths were obstructed south of present-day Swan Reach when a massive earth uplift called the Padthaway Block dammed the rivers and created the giant freshwater Lake Bungunnia. Filling over several thousand years, the lake eventually covered some 33,000 sq. km and extended north almost to today's Menindee Lakes. It survived until about 700,000 years ago, when it breached the "dam" and drained.

As Lake Bungunnia emptied, a dominant river – the Murray – began cutting a new channel across the old lake bed, incising deeply into the accumulated limestone deposits. Near Blanchetown, in SA, I saw graphic evidence of this – the Murray Gorge. A mere 400 m wide in places, with cliffs on either side, the channel confines the river from Overland Corner to Mannum.

At dusk near Blanchetown from a powerboat I watched the scalloped cliffs blaze cream, then gold, then orange as the sun set. Porous and pitted, they contain the remains of the sea creatures that once occupied the lake, life forms that Aboriginals documented in simple engravings just downstream, at the Ngaut Ngaut Conservation Park near Nildottie. There, beneath a riverfront cliff overhang blackened by countless fires, I saw images of mysterious rounded fish and estuarine dolphins that had been carved into the crumbly brown rock 6000-8000 years ago. Perhaps fossils of similar species await discovery upstream at Overland Corner, I thought, where corals, shellfish and shark teeth have already been found.

For the past 500,000 years, the Murray Basin's climate has remained mostly dry. Lower temperatures reduced evaporation from soil and water and transpiration of moisture from plants (processes known collectively as evapotranspiration). With more moisture being retained in the soil, watertables rose, wetlands formed and rivers swelled. About 60,000–40,000 years ago, the lakes and rivers of the Murray Basin were brimming with fresh water and home to an abundance of creatures.

One of the Murray's most dramatic geological eras dawned around this time when an earth movement completely changed its character for 500 km between present-day Tocumwal and Tooleybuc.

Between 300,000 and 100,000 years ago, geological upheavals had caused a vast slab of the Murray basin floor to tilt up along a geological fault line between today's towns of Deniliquin and Echuca. This fault line, called the Cadell Tilt Block (sometimes the Cadell Fault), had blocked the westward flow of both the Murray and the Goulburn rivers. However, in due course the rivers had cut through the barrier and continued their journeys, linking up further downstream.

About 50,000 years ago, another earth movement squeezed the slab up further, to a height of 12 m. This forced the Murray north and for 20,000–30,000 years flowed along the course now followed by the Edward River. The Goulburn turned south and passed through the site of present-day Echuca, joining the ancestral Murray downstream from today's Swan Hill.

Relatively recently, perhaps 8000-10,000 years ago, the Murray found a new route, flowing due south through a bottleneck to join the Goulburn near today's Echuca. This means that between Echuca and Swan Hill the Murray now flows on the bed of the ancient Goulburn.

The bottleneck along the Cadell Tilt Block could not contain high river flows, and the Murray routinely broke its banks. This overflow created a wide flood plain on which Australia's (and the world's) largest river red gum forest, referred to under the dual title of the Barmah and Millewa forests, flourishes today.

I visited the forest with wetland ecologist Keith Ward in winter. The fault line was visible as a smooth bump on the landscape as I approached from the west, but to appreciate its

full impact we motored up the 10 km bottleneck, known as The Narrows or Barmah Choke, below the Murray's junction with the Edward River just north of Echuca. Barely 35–40 m wide in places, the bottleneck was strewn with snags, but despite its low water level, the Murray still bounced along smartly. I could only imagine the scene during a flood, when the river runs a banker and flows into the crowded forest; when the red gums are up to their knees in water for weeks on end and waterbirds arrive in rowdy squadrons.

"I saw the river flow backwards here in 1993," Keith told me as we paused to contemplate how the mighty force of the flooded Murray negotiates such a tight passage. "The land's so flat that flooding downstream on the Goulburn River and Broken Creek backed the water right up the Murray to here. In the past it has backed all the way up to the Edward River."

The final chapter in the Murray's evolution began 25,000–16,000 years ago, when an ice age brought cooler, drier conditions and reduced vegetation in the Murray Basin. Evaporation increased, lakes dried out and additional salt-laden dust blew in from the west and settled in the soil and groundwater. Most significantly, other rivers flowing west from the Great Dividing Range dwindled, leaving the Murray and its major tributaries – the Lachlan, Murrumbidgee and Darling, all of which flow south – as the dominant watercourses. For most of its length, the Murray now meanders across a remarkably flat basin 500 km wide and 600 m deep, filled with the clay, sand, gravel and salt memories of its predecessors.

Changing ways

The Murray's tormented history explains much about its eccentric character. The river does not disappoint its audience; it makes five costume changes during its journey to the sea. It is a distinctly different river in its headwaters, on the riverine plains, in the SA mallee, throughout the Murray Gorge and as it empties into the lakes near its mouth.

The Murray's cradle is a moist swamp on Forest Hill, near a mountain called The Pilot in the Australian Alps. This humble birthplace is at the western extremity of the straight line that is part of the Victoria–NSW border. For 1880 km from there, the border between the two States follows the southern bank of the river (the left-hand bank as you face west), mirroring its complex meanderings until it reaches SA. This means that throughout this leg of its journey the river itself is in NSW.

Marshalling the rain and snowmelt of winter and spring, the Murray sets out on the first leg of its journey to the sea, the 350 km stretch to Albury. Before Towong, it meets the Swampy Plain River, brimming with water from power stations of the Snowy Mountains Hydro-electric Scheme (about 14 per cent of the average Murray flow at Hume Dam). East of Albury, it backs up behind Hume Weir, and, with the Mitta Mitta River, creates Lake Hume, the Murray Basin's major reservoir for regulating flows along most of the Murray. Just downstream of the dam, it meets the Kiewa River.

Beyond Corowa, the Murray weaves across riverine plains through a maze of floodplain streams, billabongs and lakes to its junction with the Wakool River, near Swan Hill.

This region contains some of the most fertile agricultural land to be found along the Murray's course, a rich legacy left by ancestral watercourses. On this reach the Murray meets its main Victorian tributaries: the Ovens, upstream of Yarrawonga; the Goulburn, upstream of Echuca; the Campaspe at Echuca; and the Loddon, upstream of Swan Hill. These four, together with the Kiewa, contribute about a third of the Murray's total inflow in an average year.

North-west of Swan Hill, the Murray enters dry mallee country. Along this stretch of the river's course, the Murravian Gulf left its most telling memorial – salt deposits and meagre soils where the hardy mallee eucalypt now predominates. The Murrumbidgee River, which contributes about 11 per cent of the Murray's water, joins it near Boundary Bend. The Darling adds another 12 per cent at its muddy junction near Wentworth.

Beyond Overland Corner, the Murray abandons its broad floodplain, with all its anabranches and billabongs, for a defined course between the limestone cliffs of the Murray Gorge, making a sharp turn south at Morgan on encountering another earthen obstacle, the Morgan Block.

In its least inspiring guise, the lower Murray flows from Mannum to the sea in a wide band of tarnished copper. South of Wellington, it discharges into Lake Alexandrina and Lake Albert before clearing the barrages and running rather unceremoniously into the Coorong and the Southern Ocean.

Geometric vineyards fringe a restored wetland at Banrock Station winery (opposite) in the SA Riverland, a 30,000 ha district covered in irrigated grape vines and citrus, fruit and nut trees that earn $530 million annually. Further downstream, in the Coorong NP (above), the Murray's aquamarine waters are brackish and support a world-class fishery prized by waterbirds and anglers alike.

RIVER PEOPLE

A spring breeze stirred the giant red gums beside the Murray just outside Albury, carrying the distant, deep-throated voice of a didgeridoo; the musician remained anonymous in the crowd. Some people in the gathering had travelled from as far away as the Northern Territory to join in the Mungabareena Ngan Girra Festival.

Moving among the throng was Cec Grant, Wiradjuri community elder, pastor and festival stalwart. Emblazoned across the back of his T-shirt were the words "Land of many rivers; look after the land and the rivers and the land and the rivers will look after you." For at least 40,000 years before European settlement, Cec's Aboriginal ancestors were the guardians of the rivers and gathered once a year near Albury to celebrate their rich bounty. Centuries later, the ritual continues.

"The rivers were spiritually very significant to Aboriginal people; they were central to the traditional ceremonies and economies, so it's only appropriate that we should continue to meet here on the Murray," Cec told me after officially welcoming the crowd.

"We are the custodians of this country; we look after it for the great creator Baiami, and the rivers are for all people, for all generations, for all time."

Just as their forebears had done, the clan groups of the Wiradjuri had come together to sing and dance, tell stories, share bush food and discuss topical issues. The aroma of barbecued cod lingered in the air while performers in traditional kangaroo-skin dress stamped the earth, wrinkled women reminisced for hours on deckchairs and ageing orators captivated children with tales of long ago.

"Some of the people used to walk 200–300 miles [320–480 km] to get here," Cec said of the ancient tradition. "They had a good time singing and dancing and eating together; they issued passports for travel between tribal areas, performed initiations and formalised marriages. And then they went up into the mountains to collect bogong moths. The moths were nutritious and the people grew fat and shiny. It was a time of renewal."

Harvesting the river's resources

Renewing ties with their land and each other is a challenge for today's Aboriginal people, most of whose ancestors were forced from their homelands by European settlers in the mid-1800s. But their long

Ethereal Yorta Yorta Dancers (opposite) Chris Thorne, Wally Cooper and his sons Kevin (kneeling) and Jesse-Lee evoke the spirit of times past at the Mungabareena Ngan Girra Festival on the banks of the Murray outside Albury. The river valley was densely populated with Aboriginal people before European settlement. Aboriginal people from southern NSW and northern Victoria gathered here every spring to conduct business and celebrate their culture before travelling into the high country to feast on bogong moths.

Cultural caretakers of Nyah State Forest Doug Nicholls, left, and Darcy Pettit proffer clay fragments used by their forebears to store heat in cooking mounds. One of the richest Aboriginal occupation sites along the Murray, the forest near Swan Hill in northern Victoria contains 120 mounds used for 200 years or more by the Wathi-Wathi and Wemba-Wemba people for hunting and gathering, and ceremonial activities.

history of occupation survives in the plentiful middens, oven mounds, artefacts, burial sites and scarred trees that dot the shores of the Murray Basin's watercourses, and it is preserved in their enduring totems, rituals and ceremonies.

For Aboriginal people, the tributaries and floodplains of the Murray River were a major food and water source, a means of transport and a repository of materials for weapons and implements, the surpluses of which could be traded. Anthropologist Radcliffe Brown, who studied Aboriginal society at the turn of the 20th century, described the Murray as "the most densely populated part of Australia before the days of white settlement". It's an assessment confirmed by Dr Colin Pardoe, president of the Australian Archaeological Association.

"The Murray is one of the core areas of Aboriginal occupation in Australia, along with the Top End and Cape York," he said of the region he has studied for more than a decade. "The river populations were large and dense, perhaps 20–40 times greater than the non-riverine populations in the same region, which were small, mobile and sparse."

In contrast to the harsh surrounding sandplain, mallee and saltbush country, the river environs were blessed with stable and abundant resources. When the waterways were flush with life, people collected the edible roots of the cumbungi, water ribbon and marsh club-rush and used reeds to make spear shafts. They dined on fish, shellfish, waterbirds and their eggs, turtles and water rats; they built ingenious weirs across creek beds to trap fish; and they fashioned nets of fibrous cumbungi roots or stringybark to snare birds. In the nearby woodlands they hunted goannas, kangaroos, possums and emus, collected berries, quandongs and other fruit and gathered seeds to grind into meal.

One of the greatest population densities occurred in an area along the Murray now reserved as Barmah State Forest and Barmah State Park, 45 km north-east of Echuca. Some of the gnarled old red gums in the 7900 ha park are more than 500 years old and would certainly have stood silent witness to the ways of the Yorta Yorta people, who plied the river in their bark canoes and made their camps on its flanking sandy outcrops. But as the trees were not about to disclose their secrets, I enlisted the help of park ranger and Yorta Yorta Aboriginal Land Council chair Leon Atkinson, a dignified man with a neatly trimmed beard and hazel eyes. Though his country was in the dry grip of winter, Leon was generous in his affection for the forest.

"Just about everything was here – water, food and medicines," he said. "We were living at the front door of our own supermarket. The Yorta Yorta never left the forest. The sights I see out here – the plants, animals, scar trees and old cooking mounds – are a constant reminder of how our mob lived. When the forest floods I throw my kids in a boat and take them cruising through the forest. They don't like the snakes too much, but you come across a lot of canoe trees that you can't normally get to."

We began by inspecting one of the forest's more easily accessible canoe trees on the 1 km Yamyabuc Discovery Trail, within cooee of the Dharnya Centre, a cultural focal point managed by Parks Victoria in conjunction with the Yorta Yorta Aboriginal community.

Leon explained that canoes were integral to the Yorta Yorta lifestyle. They served as a fishing platform and were the only means of transport during the periodic flooding.

"They used bone or a pointy stick to remove the bark, which allowed the tree to continue living," said Leon as he stroked the deep scar in the tall red gum. Unlike other Aboriginal groups, the Yorta Yorta had a ready supply of timber to draw upon. They also used the bark to fashion bowls and shields and to build huts, or mia-mias, (usually consisting of a gum-sapling frame tied together with kangaroo sinew and covered with bark). Products the Yorta Yorta didn't need they traded. "They exchanged baskets and river reeds, which made light-weight spears, for stone axes and rocks," Leon said.

Deeper in the forest we stopped in mottled shade beside Bucks Sandhill, a sandy mound encircled by fencing. Leon explained that one end of the mound was used for meetings and the other for burials. The higher ground in the forest is dotted with oven mounds, shell middens and cemeteries. Leon said he often found hand-made clay balls, blackened by fires long extinguished, that were used in the ovens to retain heat during cooking. "The mounds contain charcoal and the remains of fish, crayfish, kangaroos, emus, goannas, possums and turtles," Leon said as we concluded our short forest tour.

Images of an ancient culture

While the Aboriginals of the Murray River valley left many prosaic reminders of their presence in the landscape, they are not known for their art sites. One of the few is protected in the Ngaut Ngaut Conservation Area, 6 km downstream of Nildottie, in SA. There a towering sandstone cliff face on a broad sweep of the river speaks an ancient language.

My skin was prickling with sweat when I met Cynthia Hunter, partner of the site's custodian, Richard Hunter, beneath the scorching summer sun. It was with the greatest relief

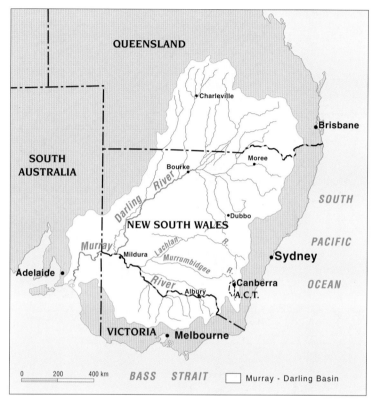

Only because Aboriginal artist Tommy McCrae sketched in pen and ink did any of his works survive the 19th century. Among them is this 1880 rendering of a traditional corroboree (left). A member of the Kwat Kwet group, Tommy lived at Lake Moodemere, near Corowa, and worked as a stockman for pioneering squatter John Foord before taking up art. He drew mostly from memory, stretched out on the ground, beginning each sketch at the bottom of the page and working his way to the top. His works, several of which are in Corowa's Federation Museum, are rare records of a culture that was fast being eroded by European contact.

that I followed her into the cool shade of a rock overhang to see some of the engravings the Nganguraku and Ngaiwong people had carved thousands of years earlier in a series of shelters. In one of the two galleries open to the public, the golden stone was alive with short-necked and long-necked turtles, fish and stick figures.

"Here you'll see the women's symbol, the sun," Cynthia said, pointing to a deep, circular pattern. "This is part of a hearth, where the women would have cooked for their families. All over the rock is evidence of a written language; the symbols show what animals can be found and when during the year. The knowledge to read these messages was oral and, sadly, much of that oral history has been lost, but the engravings bring history to life out of the cliff."

An excavation of the rock shelters in 1929–30 by South Australian Museum director Herbert Hale and anthropologist Norman Tindale was the first major dig at an Aboriginal archaeological site in Australia. Layers of ash, charcoal, bones, discarded stone implements and worn rush baskets had accumulated to a depth of more than 7 m. Radiocarbon dating confirmed that the largest of the galleries went back 8000 years and the other sites about 6000 years.

"There was clear evidence of technological development," Cynthia said. "At the lowest level were crude bone tools, then stone and improvements in stone technology before the appearance of glass – a sign of the first encounters with Europeans. Early explorers reported that there were so many Aboriginal people living along the river from Swan Reach to Mannum that their footpaths were worn in the bank."

Ngarrindjeri country

Lanky Tom Trevorrow strode off through the stunted frames of ridge-fruited and red mallee in Bonney Reserve, his mane of hair streaming in the wind. I struggled to keep pace and strained to hear his voice above the chatter of wrens and finches in the undergrowth.

"This resin could be eaten or mixed with ashes and sand to secure spearheads to their shafts," he said, pointing to the rich toffee-like sap visible on the trunk and branches of the golden wattle. "And this tea-tree was burnt to rid my people and the land of bad spirits and to cure the children of bad behaviour."

During our walk I sampled the berries of the muntry plant, resembling miniature apples but with a sharper flavour, and learnt how the Ngarrindjeri people welcomed shingleback lizards into their camps to help control insects.

Tom's bush-tucker tour is one of the highlights of a visit to Camp Coorong, the cultural, educational and recreational centre he founded 10 km south of Meningie, on the doorstep of Coorong National Park, at the Murray River's mouth. Through the purchase of an old pastoral property adjoining Bonney Reserve, used as a reserve for Ngarrindjeri people from about 1869, Tom, his brother George and community members have sought to re-establish traditional culture in their fragmented community. "It's a place for the old people to come back

to, a place we've created for ourselves, a place to feel at home in," Tom said. "Many young people are beginning to again identify with where they're from."

For centuries the Ngarrindjeri enjoyed an idyllic existence in southern SA, within easy reach of the Murray River, its freshwater lakes, the Coorong and the Southern Ocean. The fresh water provided a ready supply of waterfowl, mussels, fish, turtles, grasses and yams and the sea offered saltwater fish and shellfish and occasionally meat from stranded whales. In winter, when not even their ngowanthies (shelters) could protect them from the ocean gales, the Ngarrindjeri retreated to the mallee, where they dined on emus, kangaroos, wallabies and birdlife. "They were big, solid people, very strong and healthy because of their varied diet," said Tom, who inherits his ancestors' physical traits.

In the heart of Bonney Reserve later in the day I saw further proof, if any were needed, of the importance of Camp Coorong as a place of cultural renewal. As the setting sun gilded the low olive-green shrubs, I watched Tom's wife, Ellen, their daughter, Tanya, and Ellen's niece, Debra Rankine, demonstrate the time-honoured Ngarrindjeri art of basket-making. Sitting in a samphire-fringed saltpan, the three women were a picture of concentration. Their fingers moved nimbly as they wove the moistened reeds of the freshwater rush in a circular pattern to form neat mats. Ellen learnt the art from her aunty Dorrie just before she died and has been passing on the skill to younger women with unbridled enthusiasm ever since.

"For my old people, making baskets was a question of survival; now I'm practising it to ensure the survival of my culture," Ellen said, her plump face beaming.

Bark canoes once plied tranquil backwaters such as Gunbower Creek (above), in Gunbower State Forest, near Koondrook, in northern Victoria. Eight clans of the Barababaraba people lived in the area, leaving a legacy of scar trees, mounds and middens. Upstream, in Barmah State Park, north-east of Echuca, ranger Leon Atkinson admires a large canoe tree (opposite) from the days when his Yorta Yorta ancestors relied on bark water craft for transport. They would cure the red gum bark with fire for a short period to help with shaping and to reduce the moisture content.

The first archaeological excavations in Australia took place at Devon Downs, near this broad sweep of the Murray River at Nildottie, in southern SA. The 1929–30 studies of bones and occupation sites revealed that two distinct races of Aboriginal people, first the Negritos and then the Murrayians, occupied the Murray Valley for much longer than previously believed.

Smallpox, carried by the early European settlers, devastated the Aboriginal populations along the Coorong. George Taplin, who founded the Point McLeay Mission (now Raukkan) near Meningie in 1859, reported that Aboriginal numbers plummeted from 3200 to 511 between 1842 and 1874. Epidemics of other diseases, including measles, had preceded the arrival of settlers along the Murray River valley in the 1830s, and their impact had been just as swift and brutal.

Those who had survived soon came into conflict with the settlers when sheep and cattle overran their traditional lands. By the early 1840s most of central and western Victoria supported stock and 30,000 Europeans outnumbered the original inhabitants. The next wave of introduced ailments – respiratory infections, dysentery, syphilis and tuberculosis – took a savage toll on the dwindling Aboriginal populations. In 1857, surveyor William Blandowski was moved to write: "...I have but the most deplorable statements concerning our natives. Extermination proceeds so rapidly that the regions of the lower Murray are already depopulated, and a quietude reigns there which saddens the traveller who visited those districts a few years ago."

It's a tribute to their determination that so many Aboriginals found work along the Murray at the turn of the century as paddleboat crew members, fishermen, leech collectors, woodcutters, shepherds, trappers, shearers and seasonal workers. But by the early 1900s most were either living as fringe dwellers outside river towns or on missions. Separated from their people and their homelands, they struggled to maintain their knowledge of country and traditions. To their credit they have survived and live to tell of their culture, heritage and the history of their lands.

The Europeans arrive

"As for the Murray ever becoming an agricultural country, the idea is absurd ... there is hardly a settler on the Lower Murray who can even luxuriate in a vegetable."

Crown Lands Commissioner Evelyn Sturt was emphatic in his 1853 dismissal of the Murray valley's potential, but it was the promise of rich agricultural land that had earlier inspired his brother, the explorer Charles Sturt. The swift and largely successful European settlement that followed the favourable reports of first Hamilton Hume and William Hovell and then Charles Sturt and Thomas Mitchell in the 1820s and '30s not only proved Evelyn Sturt wrong but also established the Murray River as an economic and social artery of inland Australia.

ROONKA DISCOVERIES

One of the few Aboriginal sites along the Murray to have been excavated is at Roonka, on the river's west bank, north of Blanchetown in SA.

In 1968 South Australian Museum archaeologist Graeme Pretty found that the eroding sand dune had been occupied for the past 7500 years and used as a burial site from 5000 years ago until the period of European contact. While it is not the oldest of the Murray's Aboriginal cemeteries – upstream sites at Wallpolla and Kow Swamp are thought to go back 11,000 years – the variety of ways in which people were buried there is intriguing.

More than 200 people lay in a series of graves in the high sand dune and showed evidence of complex mortuary customs. Men and women were buried in different ways and facing different directions of the compass. One adult was buried in an animal-skin cloak and wearing a headpiece of wallaby teeth, and a child wore the remains of a bird-skull pendant.

At the time, Graeme Pretty said the practices "appear to reflect thousands of years of religious and social evolution, rather than technological evolution. At the same time it reflects the great harmony which existed between the Aboriginal people and their environment for thousands of years before the European invasion of Australia."

The site is now protected in the Roonka Conservation Park, which is closed to the public. The South Australian Museum holds the excavated skeletal remains of 150 people and a number of artefacts and grave goods with the permission of Aboriginal people from the region.

▦ A long-gone artisan with connections to the Nganguraku and Ngaiwong people created this engraving in sandstone beneath a rock overhang near Nildottie, in SA. Now preserved in the Ngaut Ngaut Conservation Park, the sun pattern, a women's symbol, features in one of two galleries dating back 8000 years. The conservation area, which includes burial sites, canoe and coolamon trees and hearths, is open to the public by arrangement.

Artist Ellen Trevorrow deftly threaded freshwater rushes native to the Lower River and the Coorong region to weave the spell of the Seven Sisters Dreaming, passed down from her Ngarrindjeri ancestors. The large circular mat symbolises the Earth; the baskets, traditionally used to carry valuable personal items, represent the seven stars known in classical mythology as the Pleiades, the seven daughters of Atlas. Ellen is reviving and maintaining the time-honoured tradition of basket-weaving at the Camp Coorong cultural centre, in the Murray's lower SA reaches.

Standing on the lush banks of the Murray at modern-day Albury, beside the now ailing red gum that Hume and Hovell blazed in 1824, I reflected on how rapid the river's conquest had been. Bark had long since obliterated the inscription in the tree, the town's oldest landmark, but around me the communities that the explorers' travels had encouraged were flourishing.

The discovery of the broad watercourse at Albury that they named the Hume was the highlight of Hume and Hovell's 2000 km, 16-week journey from Sydney to Port Phillip Bay, in Victoria. "Going sou'-west we were stopped by a river," they reported. "This beautiful stream... is serpentine, the banks clothed with verdure to the water's edge... the finest and most promising stream yet discovered in Australia..."

But despite this promise, settlement south-west of Sydney remained restricted to the Murrumbidgee River until Charles Sturt discovered the Darling in 1828 and Sturt separately embarked on an adventurous expedition down the Murrumbidgee in 1829-30. Sturt's second mission was ostensibly to identify good pastoral tracts and to solve the mystery of the Australian river system, which was long thought to converge on an inland sea.

After a brief overland journey, Sturt's nine-man party built and launched a whaleboat and began following the Murrumbidgee in the hope that it might lead them to the Darling. In January 1830 the crew were "...hurried into a broad and noble river". Passing what they rightly guessed was the Darling junction, Sturt hoisted the Union Jack and named the river on which they were travelling in honour of Sir George Murray, Secretary of State for the Colonies in the British Government. "It is impossible for me to describe the effect of so instantaneous a change of circumstances upon us," Sturt wrote of entering the Murray. "We continued to gaze in silent pleasure on the capacious channel."

The party then bobbed along the Murray for more than half its length, reaching its mouth in SA on 11 February. Observing that the river spilled into a large lake, Sturt deemed the prospects here far less promising. "...I could not but regret that the Murray had thus terminated, for I immediately foresaw that in all probability we should be disappointed in finding any practicable communication between the lake and the ocean."

The lake and the seemingly unnavigable mouth convinced them that traffic on the river would never be able to link with seaside ports such as Port Adelaide. Fatigued and starving, Sturt's party retraced its exhausting journey against the current. Fortunately, Sturt's daring effort was not without its rewards. His discovery of the Darling River and subsequent Murray explorations have been described as "the most important pieces of inland exploration in Australian history". The latter proved that the Murray was navigable and his glowing reports of the river's lower reaches inspired no less than the settlement of SA.

By 1835-36 a group of squatters had settled near Albury, not far from the blazed Hovell Tree, and graziers were looking to the west. But it was left to Major Thomas Mitchell to prove Sturt's theory that the Darling and Murray merged and to explore the Murray's middle section. In 1836 he overlanded through NSW to the Murray–Darling junction, then followed the

The abundant food and water of the lower Murray River, lakes and Coorong in SA encouraged the Ngarrindjeri people to establish more permanent settlements, unlike their mallee neighbours who moved around their land more frequently. Large hemispherical dwellings, or ngowanthie, like this one (left) on the shores of Lake Alexandrina, circa 1880, consisted of a timber frame covered with seaweed, reeds, mud and turf. The Ngarrindjeri were both accomplished fishers and basket-makers. They knotted cumbungi fibres to make intricate fishing nets, and the women fashioned a range of coiled mats, baskets and fishing scoops from native rushes. Basketry continued even after many Ngarrindjeri were forced into missions in the late 1800s; these women (below) are laden with products for sale in about 1915.

Murray upstream to its junction with the Murrumbidgee before crossing into Victoria and following the river upstream to the town he named Swan Hill. Near there, Mitchell commented: "As I stood, the first European intruder on the sublime solitude of these verdant plains, as yet untouched by flocks or herds; I felt conscious of being the harbinger of mighty changes; and that our steps would soon be followed by the men and animals for which it seemed to have been prepared."

Mitchell also saw the river's potential as a highway: "This stream was also navigable when we were there and produce might be conveyed by it at such seasons, to the sea shore". In time, Mitchell was proved prophetic and the tracks made by his wagon, known as the "Major's Line", were promptly publicised as a guide to the rich grazing country on the southern perimeters of the Murray Basin.

Some four years later Count Paul Strzelecki encountered the Murray near Corryong and followed it upstream into the mountains to chart its upper reaches. But the exact location of the river's source remained a mystery until Thomas Townsend, NSW's Deputy Surveyor-General, mapped the Murray's headwaters in 1847.

BY PERMISSION OF THE NATIONAL LIBRARY OF AUSTRALIA

■ Hamilton Hume and William Hovell, their expedition immortalised in this wood engraving of a river crossing (above) in 1825, became the first Europeans to see the Murray during their 2000 km journey from Sydney to Port Phillip Bay, in Victoria. They named it the Hume in 1824 and described vast tracts of fertile land in NSW and Victoria. Despite this, westward population expansion was limited until Captain Charles Sturt led a daring expedition down the Murrumbidgee and the Hume, which he named the Murray, by whaleboat in 1829–30. The adventure was marked by numerous threatening encounters with Aboriginals (right), but Sturt returned safely with news of a "capacious channel" and favourable settlement prospects.

Gold and growth

Once the Murray's course had been traced, the river opened up large tracts of inland Australia to settlement. The founding of SA in 1836 made available new grazing land in the river's lower reaches, and by 1838 NSW drovers were overlanding cattle beside the Murray to stock the new runs and satisfy the growing demand for meat in Adelaide.

By the end of the 1840s, squatters occupied most of the river frontage in the Murray valley, and small towns were developing at convenient river crossings. To the punt, general store and grog shanty or inn were soon added a blacksmith's shop, police station and mail service, and thus was many a community born.

But it was the discovery of gold – first at Ophir, near Orange in 1851, then at Bendigo, Beechworth, Adelong, Peak Hill, Sofala and Hill End – that fostered the growth of the small river towns, since rivers offered the quickest access to the mines. Around the goldfields, settlers identified both promising grazing land and commercial opportunities, and when the gold was exhausted some stayed.

However, one of the most significant impacts of the frenetic activity at the diggings was on forms of transport. Most of the bullockies who had hitherto been servicing the riverland stations were lured by the prospect of the shorter, more lucrative runs between the goldfields and the growing settlements. Their departure stranded many of the remoter river settlements and stations; in the Riverina and along the Darling River, squatters soon began to run out of essential foods and were forced to stockpile their wool clip. Another means of transport had to be found, and fast.

STATE LIBRARY OF NEW SOUTH WALES

An inland highway is born

As I sat on the weathered, three-tiered wharf at Echuca, gazing at the Murray's khaki waters, historian Helen Coulson told stories of the port's colourful history and the role it played in easing the isolation of inland settlements. Afternoon sunlight danced on the river and a steady stream of boats paraded past. Among them was the *Alexander Arbuthnot*, the last traditional paddle-steamer built on the Murray-Darling system, which announced its approach with a breathy blast of its whistle. With so many craft jostling for berths on the restored wharf, it wasn't hard to imagine the scene, more than a century earlier, when Echuca really hummed.

"This wharf was 332 m long, with a log slip at one end, seven cranes – two of them 10-tonnes – and a woolshed," Helen said proudly. "There were five railway lines heading into the port side by side, coming and going. It was a frantic time. In the 1880s some £2 million worth of produce passed through it annually. Echuca was the second most important port in Victoria and the focal point of river traffic, funnelling trade by rail to Melbourne."

Although arguably the most notable, Echuca was just one of a number of river ports and boat-building centres, including Wahgunyah, Mildura, Wentworth, Morgan and Goolwa, that beaded the Murray. Capable of probing deep into the inland along the Murray and

▥ Studded with pelicans and other waterbirds, the junction of the Murray and Darling rivers at Wentworth is a picture of serenity that belies its importance in the Murray–Darling Basin system. Fed by monsoonal rain falling in southern Queensland and north-eastern NSW, the 2740 km Darling and its tributaries contribute some 12 per cent of the Murray's inflows. At the turn of the century it guaranteed the Murray significant river commerce, most notably the transport of the wool clip from sheep stations in the north. Nearly 100 paddle-steamers worked the Darling in the 1890s, when Wentworth wharf and its customs house were a hive of activity. Charles Sturt named the Murray not far from this confluence in January 1830.

Gold discoveries in northern Victoria in the 1850s fostered the growth of scores of towns along the Murray. Scenes like this at Eaglehawk near Bendigo (below) were common as small settlements sprouted on the diggings. When the gold ran out, many miners stayed to capitalise on the riverfront grazing and commercial opportunities. Tocumwal grew up as a river crossing in 1862, offering facilities such as the Terminus Hotel (right) to service the pioneering wool and grain producers.

APPROACH TO EAGLE HAWK FROM ROAD T

BY PERMISSION OF THE
NATIONAL LIBRARY OF AUSTRALIA

The last authentic riverboat built on the Murray, the PS *Alexander Arbuthnot* (opposite left) is today a showpiece of the historic port of Echuca, once the largest inland port in Australia but hard-hit by declining river trade. The impact of the decline was less painful upstream at Tocumwal (opposite right), which revived during World War II as a base for the US Army Air Corps and the RAAF.

its tributaries, the riverboats played a crucial role in opening up southern and western NSW, northern Victoria, SA and even southern Queensland. They could transport people and goods more simply and cheaply than bullock teams and offered new, convenient access to capital cities and world markets.

The era of steam navigation dawned on the Murray–Darling system in 1853. By 1870, 200 paddle-steamers, crewed by "inside sailors" or "mud pirates", as they were called, were operating for about eight months of the year along 5000–7000 km of rivers.

The vessels varied in size and shape, depending on where they were used and for what purpose. Generally they were of sturdy timber-and-iron construction, double-decked and powered by wood-fired steam engines. They were broad of beam, with shallow draughts of between 60 cm and 1.2 m, and sported two side-wheels for manoeuvrability. They were generally 15–35 m long by 3–8 m wide and towed barges that carried an average of 1200 bales of wool stacked five or six high.

The early boats were noisy and were redolent of oil, wood and steam. They belched clouds of smoke and at night sparks erupted like fireworks from their stacks. Children could recognise the paddleboats by the sound of their whistles, the thrash of their paddlewheels or their smoke plumes.

The river level would fall late in the year, and unless there was abnormal rain, it didn't begin to rise again until the winter rains fell on the headwaters. In most years the river was so low that larger vessels had to tie up and wait for the next "rise", and only those boats with the shallowest draughts could continue operating.

As well as carrying stores and cargo such as timber and wool (the main commodity), the steamers were used for commercial fishing, towing other boats, desnagging the river and conveying everyone from midwives to men of the cloth. The mission steamer *Etona*, for instance, ferried Archdeacon Bussell to isolated station landings where he conducted baptisms, births and marriages. Roving seamstresses aboard the *Emily Jane* would measure up customers while travelling upstream and deliver the completed garments on returning downstream. Crowded with boats from the 1860s to 1900, its heyday as a waterway, the Murray came to be known as the "Mississippi of Australia".

However, the development of rail and motor transport networks conspired against the river trade at the turn of the century. Governments intent on promoting rail services offered lower freight rates and strictly enforced customs regulations and duties, undermining the profitability of the paddle-steamers. Although the steamboat companies fought valiantly to remain in business, they were hindered by the severe drought of 1914–15 and the outbreak of World War I, which drained the wharves and boats of workers. Save for a few timber transports, the riverboats had all but disappeared from the Murray by the 1930s.

STEAMING INTO HISTORY

The river trade owes its origins to an entrepreneurial flour merchant, his desire to build a trading steamer and the temptation of a cash prize. The merchant was William Randell, the son of a wealthy miller. Although he had no sailing or boating experience, he was far-sighted enough to see the river's potential as a trade artery.

In the early 1850s Randell and his brothers, Thomas and Elliott, began building the wooden steamer *Mary Ann* at Noa-No Landing, near Mannum. He had not heard that in 1850 the SA Government, keen to inspire the development of river transport, had offered £2000 to each of the first two iron steamers to cover the 818 km from Goolwa to the Darling River junction. Randell had his eye on other prizes – new markets in the fledgling settlements along the river for his family's business, in particular the recently discovered Ovens goldfield.

Skippered by Randell, the *Mary Ann*, "a very unpleasant vessel to travel in, making an excessive noise", set out from Goolwa in March 1853, becoming the first steamer to ply the Murray. However, about 42 km above the site of Morgan, SA, low water forced Randell to return to Mannum to wait for the river to rise.

Meanwhile, an astute and experienced ocean sailor named Francis Cadell was readying his iron steamer, the *Lady Augusta*, with an eye on the cash prize. He left Goolwa in August 1853, the month in which the rising river allowed Randell to resume his journey from Mannum.

When Cadell arrived at Euston on 13 September, he heard that the *Mary Ann* had passed through there the day before. Cadell gave chase at once, the quest now being to see who could get furthest upstream.

Cadell overtook a startled Randell above the Murrumbidgee junction the following day. Over the next three days the boats overtook each other several times, "snags clutching at their sides and boilers fit to burst".

On September 17, Swan Hill's entire population – 15 Aboriginals, 10 white men and two white women – turned out to greet the *Lady Augusta*. The *Mary Ann* steamed in three hours later.

Cadell received the entire £4000 prize and although Randell was not officially eligible to receive any money, public subscription raised a consolation prize for him. The two men had proved that the Murray was navigable by large vessels and both remained involved for many years in the river trade they helped inspire.

Captain Francis Cadell (far right) collected a cash prize for becoming, in 1853, the first to take an iron steamer – the LADY AUGUSTA, pictured towing her barge EUREKA – upstream from Goolwa. He and William Randell, aboard the MARY ANN, proved that navigation of the Murray was commercially viable. The era of river transport peaked in 1870–80.

The deserts bloom

As river trade died, another major enterprise took its place. Today the legacy of the rather chequered beginnings of irrigation farming on the Murray can be seen on the fertile flats around Mildura, in north-western Victoria. Known as the Sunraysia region, it produces 95 per cent of Australia's dried vine fruits, one-third of our citrus and one-third of our wine grapes. During my visit there I surveyed a landscape resembling a grid map – vineyards, citrus and almond groves, and vegetable fields studded with asparagus, melons and avocados, all drinking from the Murray River.

At the turn of the century, people around the world were encouraged to migrate to Mildura, a region so bountiful that "it will grow anything; just add water", to take part in an ambitious irrigation initiative proposed by George and William (Ben) Chaffey. These Canada-born brothers had founded successful irrigation colonies in the United States. In 1887, enticed by the then Victorian Minister for Water Supply, Alfred Deakin, they established Australia's first irrigation schemes, initially at Renmark, in SA, then at Mildura, in Victoria.

But the 400 battlers who invested in Mildura grew tense when they saw the first signs of salinisation, started losing large amounts of water from their irrigation channels to evaporation, and distant markets posed delivery problems. Some refused to pay the water charges, and for many the 1890s depression was the last straw. Financially crippled, the Chaffey brothers were themselves declared bankrupt in 1895.

A year later, the establishment of the First Mildura Irrigation Trust launched the cooperative irrigation movement on the Murray. It was a model later adopted in SA. The governments realised that irrigation could boost the river's development and agreed to support the establishment of cooperative village settlements. Their literature spoke glowingly of "deserts blooming" in a "Garden of Eden". But the reality was very different. Many settlements struggled because the farmers had little agricultural experience or were unwilling to cooperate.

The pace of irrigation development at Renmark was slower, but because this was a smaller settlement (just 66 investors) than the one at Mildura, it did not require the same degree of pioneering effort. It had better transport facilities and a more reliable water supply (it had the Darling as well as the Murray to draw from) and was thus easier to manage. But the Renmark Irrigation Trust also suffered through the mid-1890s bank crash, and it, too, crumbled. However, like Mildura, it recovered when circumstances improved in the early 1900s.

Irrigation projects large and small continued both to flounder and prosper along the river and its tributaries. Experimentation with socialistic village settlements continued in SA and Victoria, and soldier settlement schemes were actively promoted after both world wars. The key to success was a reliable water supply, which the Murray River of the day, prone to erratic variations in flow, could not guarantee. The call soon went up for surety of supply, and the River Murray Commission answered with an enormous construction program aimed at taming the unpredictable rivers.

STATE LIBRARY OF NEW SOUTH WALES

Canada-born brothers William "Ben" Chaffey (above left) and George (above right) helped develop Australia's first irrigation colonies at Renmark and Mildura in the late 1880s. They relied on the 1888 prospectus *The Australian Irrigation Colonies Illustrated* (below), also called *The Red Book*, to entice migrant settlers to buy irrigated blocks as they were opened up, thereby financing the expansion of engineering works. But investment and enthusiasm were no match for salinisation, evaporation from irrigation channels and transport problems.

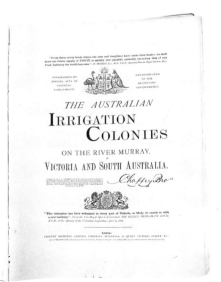

THE GREAT PROVIDER

"It's almost criminal to be out on a day like today and be paid for it."

Hydrographer Rod Kerr was speaking as he prepared to launch his shallow-draught boat in the turbid Murray near Albury.

"But it's not always like this," he added. "Sometimes it's bad weather, a rising river, with snags floating down and the prospect of being cut off for two days by floodwaters. It's all part of the job."

I'd met Rod and hydrographic assistant Mark Dicketts at Doctors Point, immediately downstream of the Murray's junction with the Kiewa River and 12 km below Hume Dam. It was a morning in early winter and a light breeze ruffling the water had sent Rod racing for his beanie. Cattle grazed contentedly on the Victorian side of the Murray as Rod and Mark slid their craft into the river at one of the river's principal gauging stations.

"These stations are strategically placed to measure the inflow and diversions from the Murray," explained Rod. "We take a minimum of 15 depth and velocity measurements across the stream; the width and depth give the area and then I multiply that by the velocity to get a flow measurement. It's a never-ending process because rivers are always changing."

As the NSW Department of Land and Water Conservation hydrographer for the upper Murray, Rod is responsible for taking regular measurements at 29 such gauging stations. The data he gathers is used by the Murray–Darling Basin Commission, the manager of the Murray River and its tributaries, to make informed decisions on water releases from the system's main storages – releases that ensure water quality and that environmental, irrigation and water supply needs are met.

"It's a constant balancing act," Rod said. "Whenever we manipulate the river there are consequences and some of them we are painfully aware of. I constantly marvel at the idiosyncrasies of the Murray. It's a dynamic medium. People tend to think of rivers in static terms, but I've picked up the pulses in the river's flow. Surges move downstream and the water travels like a wave."

Modern technology has ensured that hydrographers like Rod have a much better understanding of the Murray's rhythm today, but historically it was an unpredictable force. Before being impounded by dams and weirs, the Murray had a seasonal cycle of high flows in spring and low flows in late summer and autumn. In flood years, it would fan out across the floodplain; in dry years it sometimes shrank to a string of pools.

▥ Temporary emerald isles (opposite) support a sprinkling of sheep on the Victorian side of the Murray in its upper reaches near Lake Hume. Descending from the Australian Alps, the Murray is captured by the 20,190 ha lake and its flow is carefully manipulated to meet irrigation, water supply, electricity generation and recreational needs. Irrigation releases are greatest in the December–March period.

▓ Hydrographer Rod Kerr and hydrographic assistant Mark Dicketts gauge the Murray's flow (above) downstream of its confluence with the Kiewa River at Doctors Point, near Albury. By measuring the distance along the gauging wire, as well as depths and velocities beneath it, they can calculate how much water the river is carrying. Rod's downstream counterpart, Paul Cleaver (right), takes similar measurements near Barmah, in northern Victoria. A network of computerised gauging stations monitors the flows of the Murray and its tributaries, but additional hydrographic data is vital to take account of transmission losses, inflows from tributaries, and diversions. This information helps Murray–Darling Basin Commission staff make daily estimates of how much water is available in the river system for equitable sharing and it also helps with the management of natural events so that adverse impacts of floods and droughts are kept to a minimum.

Water was diverted from the river for small-scale irrigation soon after European settlement, but it was the riverboat captains' desire for year-round travel that prompted the first discussions about building locks on the Murray. An inter-colonial conference in 1863 concluded "that the commerce, population, and wealth of Australia can be largely increased by rendering navigable and otherwise utilising the great rivers of the interior such as the Murray, Edward, Murrumbidgee and Darling".

However, several obstacles had to be overcome before such an ambition could be achieved. Two of the greatest were political pig-headedness and procrastination. Rivalry over customs duties, navigation and irrigation ambitions meant the NSW, Victorian and SA governments could not agree on sharing the water. This antagonism was brought home to me when I visited the Corowa district, just west of Albury. Standing by the old Wahgunyah customs house, across the river from Corowa, the president of the Corowa District Historical Society,

Spilling lazily across the landscape, the Murray arm of Lake Hume is a maze of channels (above) upstream from Albury. The lake is practical as well as beautiful: it is one of four storages, 14 weirs and five barrages built to regulate the Murray to ensure that the water needs of three States – NSW, Victoria and SA – are satisfied.

Until he retired recently, affable storage officer Barry Halpin, pictured in the colonnade on the Hume Dam wall, had the job of overseeing the Hume Weir's operation and maintenance.

Glenda Campbell, told me the vexing inter-colonial trade disputes had spilled over into violence and arrests at this humble brick building, reinforcing the call for Federation.

"Long-standing bitterness over the payment of customs duties was the impetus for the Federation conference in Corowa in July 1893," Glenda told me. The then Premier of Victoria, James Patterson, made his views clear, declaring: "When a man who comes here from Victoria is regarded as a foreigner and a woman who goes to Wahgunyah treated as a smuggler, liable to be stuck up by a policeman and customs officer, it is time some change was made." The more conciliatory SA Governor of the day, Richard MacDonnell, remarked that though the Murray River divided the colonies of Victoria and NSW, "it flows for all of us, and unites us all closely together".

Glenda explained that the resolution passed by delegates at the Corowa conference outlined the means of achieving Federation and served as the foundation for the Australian Constitution, but agreement on the contentious issue of water entitlements was a long time coming. A series of savage droughts between 1895 and 1902, several State royal commissions and then the Corowa water conference of 1902 ushered in a new era of cooperation on water issues. Delegates agitating for protection against drought agreed that a Royal Commission needed to investigate "the conservation and distribution of the Murray and its tributaries for the purposes of irrigation, navigation and water supply".

It wasn't until 1915, after more than a decade of stagnation and negotiation and the droughts of 1913–14, that the River Murray Waters Agreement was reached between the Commonwealth and NSW, Victoria and SA on how the river's waters should be managed and shared. The agreement set up the River Murray Commission (the precursor of today's Murray–Darling Basin Commission) to establish how water requirements would be met through the construction of storages, locks and weirs.

Taming the rivers

The concrete spillway at Hume Weir suddenly spluttered to life. At first there was only a fine spray, but as the four cavernous valves continued to open, white plumes thundered into the depths of the Murray River channel 16 km upstream of Albury. Cormorants and gulls were quickly on the scene, attracted by the prospect of an easy meal of dazed fish. They fluttered above the froth, unperturbed by the roar.

Storage officer Barry Halpin watched the flow impassively. It was a familiar sight to him, but one he has never tired of in 41 years of working at the dam. Water, after all, is the giver of life, he said.

When full, Lake Hume holds 3 million megalitres (compared with Sydney Harbour's half-million) and is the most critical operational water storage in the entire Murray River system. It captures rainwater that falls within a 15,300 sq. km catchment, including the Murray River's headwaters in the Australian Alps, the Mitta Mitta River (via Dartmouth Reservoir) and the Snowy River and its tributary, the Eucumbene.

ALBURY & DISTRICT HISTORICAL SOCIETY

■ Seventeen years in the making (left), Hume Dam was officially completed in 1936, guaranteeing a year-round supply of water from the Murray catchment by storing high winter flows and releasing them in the drier summer months. The dam was enlarged to its present capacity in 1961. Discharges for irrigation today (below) – a maximum of 25,000 megalitres daily – usually begin in early September and continue until early May.

As Barry and I watched the spectacle, he had to raise his voice above the din to explain that the dam acts as a form of insurance, storing the late-winter and spring rainfall until it is needed. Lake Hume forms part of a system of structures managed by River Murray Water, the business unit of the MDBC that manages the Murray system. In addition to the Hume and Dartmouth storages, it controls three others – Lake Mulwala, Menindee Lakes and Lake Victoria – 16 weirs that pool the Murray River from Torrumbarry to Blanchetown, and the Edward River and lower Murrumbidgee River, and five barrages near the river's mouth.

Water is diverted from the Murray and its tributaries throughout the year for irrigation, homes and farms, though demand increases after August and culminates in a peak from December to March. "To manage the Murray we turn the taps on and off all the way up the river," Barry said. "And we're the last call here at Hume, the big tap before the big tank."

It's a delicate balancing act of continually lowering and topping up the major water storages. MDBC staff use computer models to estimate how much water needs to be released and from where, relying on information gathered by gauging stations and hydrographers like Rod Kerr. These estimates are adjusted daily to allow for losses along the way, inflows from tributaries and forecast diversions.

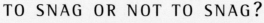

TO SNAG OR NOT TO SNAG?

From the 1960s to 1987, almost 115,000 fallen trees, called snags, were hauled out of the Murray River between Lake Hume and Lake Mulwala alone. The aim was to aid water flow, improve navigation, ensure the safety of recreational users and reduce flooding. However, in the early 1990s desnagging was dramatically curtailed and now some researchers are campaigning for snags to be replaced.

This complete about-face reflects growing awareness of how river regulation and intervention affect native plant and animal species. We now know that snags provide shelter for aquatic plants and invertebrates, roosts for waterbirds, feeding sites for animals such as water rats, and basking sites for a variety of creatures, including turtles. In water deeper than 50 cm, where there's less light, snags serve as collection points for debris that sustains micro-organisms and supports dense populations of nematodes and fungi, which are in turn grazed by prawns and shrimps.

For fish like callop, trout cod and Murray cod, snags are invaluable. they provide a refuge from predators, sunlight and fast water, a spawning site and feeding ground, and may also define territories.

In his report, *Fish Need Trees*, John Koehn, principal scientist in freshwater ecology at Victoria's Arthur Rylah Institute for Environmental Research, wrote: "Snags are as vital to cod as trees are to birds... Had this number of trees been cut down along the riverbanks there would have been a massive public outcry at the loss of terrestrial habitat sites for birds, mammals, etc. The effect of this habitat destruction on the cod populations was not measured, but it is likely that such a massive loss of habitat has led to a proportional reduction in fish numbers."

To strike a balance today, only those snags considered a major obstruction to flow or navigation are removed, and many are left below the water level.

Vanishing mist reveals a moody stretch of river strewn with snags near Tocumwal, in southern NSW. Long considered obstructions to river flow and boating and recreational hazards, snags were only recently recognised for their environmental virtues. As well as serving as "parking bays" for fish, habitat for aquatic invertebrates, and bird roosts and feeding sites, they are now known to collect debris on which many microscopic animals feed.

A verdant corridor survives the summer harvester in a freshly baled hay paddock near Bethanga on Lake Hume. Across more than 1 million sq. km the Murray–Darling Basin accounts for 41 per cent of the gross value of Australia's agricultural production and is often dubbed the "food basket of the nation". Cropping, horticulture and livestock production are the main agricultural activities.

■ With a complexion as ruddy as his ripe peaches, fruit-grower Glen Weinert (above) is well pleased with his crop at Waikerie, in the SA Riverland. His 3 ha irrigated "fruit-salad farm" also produces mangos, avocados, apricots, youngberries, oranges and mandarins, which are either sold locally or through the Adelaide markets. Waikerie is the largest citrus-growing and packing region in the State. Citrus is also favoured on a smaller scale upstream near Cobram, in northern Victoria, where the Murray (opposite) snakes through dense redgum forest. Irrigation is easiest on the Murray's fertile riverine plains between Corowa and Swan Hill, where the lie of the land allows gravity-fed delivery. It is also in this section that the Murray meets its main Victorian tributaries: the Ovens, Goulburn, Campaspe and Loddon rivers. With the Kiewa upstream, they contribute about one-third of the Murray's total flow in an average year.

As one of three storage officers at Hume Weir, Barry appreciates better than most the demands of managing such capricious resources and the hard yakka that went into building the dams that contain them. He started work at the dam in 1957 as a member of the steel gang that bent steel and tied reinforcements for the dam's rising superstructure. He left for a temporary stint as a railway conductor before returning as a jackhammer operator and later becoming involved in instrumentation.

"I grew up with the job," he said as he proudly showed me the greystone quarry from which most of the weir's stone was cut. "I worked on most stages of the expansion; we often worked seven days a week, sometimes 16 hours a day. I just like the place – I must have, to come back to it – and I ended up with the job I wanted."

But Barry is the first to admit that the challenges and responsibilities are often immense. "It's fairly intense during a flood, especially," he said. "You can be recording inflows every hour or half-hour, depending on the amount of rain and the rise you're getting in the storage. We can't have any more water going out than is coming in. There's a real buzz about the place when we're in full flight. A good flood helps keep you in tune."

Slaking a growing thirst

The citrus harvest was in full swing when I toured the sculpted fields of the Curlwaa Irrigation Scheme, in the far south-western corner of NSW across the river from Mildura. Squat trees dripped with bright orange and yellow fruit, and young grapevines straggled up through the red earth, creating a neat lattice design across the flat landscape. My eloquent guide, scheme director and vice-chairman Col Thomson, a cultured gentleman with a thick shock of dark hair, appeared glad of the break from picking navel oranges when I called in at his 33 ha citrus farm, enclosed by a bend in Tuckers Creek. "You've got to be flexible to survive in farming these days," he said.

Curlwaa, Col explained, is a prime example of agricultural innovation. Although now privatised and part of Western Murray Irrigation, in 1888 it became the first government irrigation area to be established in NSW. Initially Murray water reached the fledgling orchards that were emerging in the district in channels dug in the soil.

During the 1920s the irrigation channels were concreted and the land furrowed so that crops could be irrigated by flooding. But the farmers were generous with the water and the channels leaked. Water then seeped deep into the soil, gradually raising the watertable until it reached ancient salt deposits. As the water, already naturally salty, rose through these deposits, it picked up and dissolved more salt and brought it to the soil's surface, a process known as salinisation.

Signs of salinisation stopped everyone in their tracks in the 1930s. Farmers realised they needed better channels to help reduce the waterlogging. Fifty years later, the association of 100 farming families in the 1107-hectare Curlwaa Irrigation Scheme replaced all their irrigation channels with 30 km of underground pipes.

Like flickering windmills, Murray-fed sprinklers spray orchards near Tocumwal, in southern NSW. Enterprising farmers began pumping from the river on a small scale in the late 1800s, but irrigation expanded rapidly after World War I, once political negotiations and the subsequent regulation of the river guaranteed a regular water supply. Returning soldiers were often given a fresh start in the fledgling Government-managed irrigation schemes, and by 1928 some 2630 sq. km of crops were being watered along the Murray. This has grown to about 7300 sq. km.

"You won't see an open channel anywhere today; it's all underground in cement and PVC [polyvinyl-chloride] pipes. All our pumps are computer-controlled and most of the farmers are converting to microsprinklers," Col said. "The channel system was losing about 30 per cent of the water it carried through evaporation and seepage. We've seen the watertable drop 2–3 m in 10 years as a result of these measures. Environmentally it's been phenomenal."

But perhaps the district's most impressive measure affecting the Murray's health can be found 5 km from Col's home. On the outskirts of Curlwaa, where the irrigated fields abruptly meet the dead-flat saltbush plains that stretch to Broken Hill, Col showed me how farmers are dealing with the 4500–5000 tonnes of salt carried from their fields by leached irrigation water each year, often generated by overwatering.

Shimmering in the distance was Fletcher Lake, a rapidly diminishing bowl of water rimmed by salt encrustations and dusty saltbush and bluebush. Col explained that, since the 1960s, all water draining from irrigated fields in Curlwaa and the adjoining Coomealla district is pumped to the lake and allowed to evaporate. "The lake is not something to be proud of, but at least that salty water is no longer running into the river," he said.

This strategy is being used increasingly throughout the Murray–Darling Basin to combat salinisation, the greatest threat to its $10 billion agricultural industry. The post-World War II land-clearing boom, coupled with widespread irrigation, has come at a considerable cost, and nowhere is this more evident than in SA.

ENOUGH IS ENOUGH

By the early 1990s, the rivers of the Murray–Darling Basin were in a sorry state. Salinity was increasing while the health of native fish, wetlands and river red gums was declining. As well, a frightening 1000 km blue-green algal bloom had burgeoned on the Darling River. In the 50 years to 1994, the amount of water extracted from the basin's rivers for urban, industrial and agricultural use had more than tripled and they were literally running out of water.

In 1997 the Ministerial Council of the Murray–Darling Basin Commission took an extraordinary decision: it limited diversions from the rivers to 1993–94 levels by imposing a permanent "cap". It was the first time in history that limits had been permanently placed on diversions from these rivers.

The aim of "the cap", as it is commonly known, is to arrest the decline in river health by striking a balance between the economic and social benefits of water diversions and their environmental costs. Landholders have had their water allocations reduced in many regions to prevent diversions topping the 1993–94 levels as "sleeper" licences (those water allocations not used in the past) are activated. Few landholders now get the full allocation entitled to them under their water licence, and they may suffer further restrictions during dry seasons.

While the cap has been criticised by thirsty irrigators, the MDBC believes it will help guarantee secure supplies and fewer long-term problems from waterlogging and soil and river salinisation in the future.

Further agricultural expansion in the basin will now be possible only if water is used more efficiently or if water licences that give monetary value to this scarcest of resources can be traded, an increasingly popular option.

Salt-encrusted Ramco Lagoon, its red gums killed by salt leaching from surrounding slopes, serves as a warning of the consequences of inefficient irrigation practices near Waikerie, in the SA Riverland. High salinities and the increasing degradation of the Murray–Darling Basin rivers prompted the authorities to impose a cap on water diversions in the 1990s.

▦ "Irrigation is becoming a more exact science," said Paringa fruit-grower Mike Trautwein, shown trellising young mid-red plums on his 50 ha stone-fruit and wine-grape property near the SA–Victoria border. Efficient under-vine sprinklers deliver his irrigation water and a computer determines the precise water needs of individual sections of his plantings. South Australian farmers have been at the forefront of irrigation advances, partly inspired by adversity: the Murray water they inherit from the eastern States is often infused with salt resulting from natural saline inflow, bad irrigation techniques and extensive land clearing; their own soils are shallow and naturally high in salts; and SA's annual rainfall is low.

Not only do South Australians have to contend with an increasingly salty Murray as it nears the sea, but their land is also the most naturally rich in salt deposits, the legacy of the ancient seawater intrusions. As the Murray courses through the hot, dry mallee country near the SA border, saline groundwater flowing into the river, and to a lesser extent evaporation, concentrates its salty burden. If rainfall is low, there is little prospect of dilution. The State's own past inefficient irrigation and drainage practices have only compounded the problem.

At Loxton, 40 km south of Renmark in SA's Riverland, I met Tony Sharley, program leader of Primary Industries and Resources within the Murray–Darling Basin. I wanted to see the extent of the salinity problem and learn what growers in his State were doing about it.

"By the time the Murray enters South Australia, on average it is carrying a salt load of 4600 tonnes a day," Tony said, grim-faced. "Through a combination of inefficient irrigation, ponding of water in the river channel in weir pools and natural salt inflows we have been forcing about another 1470 tonnes of salt a day into the river system before Lock 9 (at Kulnine and Morgan)."

English poet Lord Byron wrote: "Till taught by pain, men really know not what good water's worth." It's been a painful lesson indeed for South Australians, but it has served to motivate growers like second-generation Italo-Australian Sam Albanese, vice-chairman of the Pike Mundic Irrigators' Association.

Sam's father toiled for years to clear the mallee after World War II to make way for the family's 47 ha of citrus trees and grapevines, and Sam's not about to jeopardise the business through poor practices. He and his family were among the first farmers in the Riverland region to have a complete soil survey done, showing what his soil could support and how much water his plants needed. Soil moisture probes help him determine precisely where and how much water to apply.

"What we are doing here has a large bearing on what happens downstream," Sam said as we walked among his leafy shiraz vines, not far from Tony Sharley's office. "The Murray River is our lifeline and there's a great benefit for all of us in working together. The idea is for us to be here in 50 years time and still have quality water."

Strapping Mike Trautwein, on a nearby stone-fruit and wine-grape property, has invested $120,000 in more efficient irrigation monitoring devices and plans to commit another $80,000. "We understand a lot more about water use on our crops these days," he said. "We have always had salt problems, and because we have marginal soil types, we've always had to be conscious of water use."

Tony Sharley is confident the collective actions of growers like Sam and Mike will reap substantial rewards, not just for them, but for the whole river community. "We estimate that with the initiatives that are going on now – irrigator training programs and irrigators becoming more efficient by modifying their irrigation systems – we will halve the volume of salt going into the river," he said.

"It may take 20 or 30 years but there's a lot we can do to reduce the impact we're having."

Fields of ripe canola under harvest resemble a woodcut design (left) at Tintaldra station, between Tintaldra and Towong, in the upper Murray Valley. The crop covers almost 10 per cent of the 1400 ha property, which has been in the Mackinnon family for three generations and relies heavily on Murray water. "You never take the river for granted," said manager Alex Mackinnon. Second-generation Italo-Australian fruit-grower Sam Albanese (below), pictured among packing cases with his children, Isabella, 6, and Dominic, 5, shares this view. His farm at Pike River, near Paringa, east of Renmark in SA, is a shining example of sound environmental practices.

GIVER OF LIFE

The small billabong wore a skirt of drying reeds and vivid sedges, embroidered with emerald duckweed. Terry Hillman waded thigh-deep across it, net in hand, his balding head and bearish frame reflected perfectly in the still surface. Now and then he paused to scoop the net through the water and pulled it close to his freckled face to examine the contents. It was a leisurely afternoon when time was measured not by the ticking of clocks but the measured barking of frogs.

We were no more than 5 km from the Murray River near Albury in an ancient arm of the watercourse. With the onset of summer, smaller backwaters had shrunk to swamps, but Ryans 2, as this well-studied pool is known, was full and brimmed with life.

At every scoop Terry recited the names of the insects and other tiny creatures he'd discovered grazing on the mossy liverwort – algae, backswimmers and a host of other creatures among them.

"I love floodplains," he said. "I know the Murray's billabongs better than I know most people in Albury. I like the fact that they contain all these poor little critters that don't show off and nobody knows are there but which are fundamental to the health of the river system."

An ecologist and director of the Murray–Darling Freshwater Research Centre in Albury, Terry has worked for more than 20 years investigating ways to ensure the sustainable management of the Murray River. The billabongs scattered like gems along the river's floodplains – those flat, flood-prone flanges of land on the river's margins – have become his particular passion.

Though 5–10 km from the river in places, these odd-shaped pools are critical to the health of the main channel, and vice versa. The billabongs are rich in organic material and the microscopic plants and animals that convert this material into energy. "In summer the bacteria break down organic matter at the same rate as a sewage treatment works; the billabongs are really bubbling," Terry said.

When the river breaks its banks and washes across the floodplain, it flushes the billabongs and ephemeral lakes with fresh water that carries with it new seeds, plant and animal species, nutrients and oxygen. For their part, the billabongs act like kidneys, trapping the floodwater's sediments, filtering out pollutants and releasing their own nutrients into the river when the floodwaters recede. By storing floodwater and releasing it gradually, the billabongs and associated wetlands also mitigate the effects of flooding.

▓ Shimmering in the late afternoon sun, Ryans 2 billabong (opposite) near Hume Dam, east of Albury, comes under the scrutiny of ecologist Terry Hillman, director of the Murray–Darling Freshwater Research Centre. "It's a matter of holding the river and floodplains in respect and trying to understand what they need," he said of his 20-year mission to ensure their sustainable management.

Before human intervention, the plants and animals in both the river and billabongs on the floodplain were attuned to alternating periods of flood and drought. Floods stimulate some fish to migrate upstream to spawn. Callop (golden perch) and silver perch breed successfully only in flood years, as long as temperatures are high enough, and short-lived species like rainbowfish and carp gudgeon spawn more intensely during a flood. Whether or not spawning is provoked by flooding, the fingerlings of virtually all the Murray's 36 fish species rely on food from wetlands – especially microinvertebrates – and in some cases the shelter they provide in their vulnerable first months of life.

But the situation for billabongs like Ryans 2 changed dramatically when the river's natural flows were manipulated. Levees built to stop the Murray flowing onto floodplains that had been reclaimed for settlements and farmland prevented floodwater from reaching the billabongs. The carefully managed river was no longer permitted to dry out in summer and floods became less frequent. Some billabong creatures today rarely experience the right conditions to regenerate and reproduce.

"One of the reasons I started working on billabongs was that I thought they were under threat," Terry told me as we inspected the slimy green contents of his net. "I've gradually come round to the view that it's the river that's at risk and it's because we've changed the way the river and its floodplain billabongs interact."

In its natural state, the Murray overflowed its banks in winter and spring and receded in summer and autumn, sometimes contracting to a necklace of pools. Under today's regulated system, water storages upstream fill during winter and spring, holding back the water until the peak irrigation period in summer and autumn, virtually reversing the natural flow upstream of the major irrigation offtakes. Most wetlands between Lake Hume and Echuca are flooded throughout the summer – the time when they would normally be drying out.

Restoring the natural balance

The aroma of damp earth filled my nostrils as I wandered out onto the chocolate-coloured bed of Moira Lake. Where the bed had dried out completely it had split into thumb-wide cracks several centimetres deep. Freshwater mussels had burrowed deep into the mud beneath to await the next flood, but even there they were not safe from determined water rats, which had left the shell leftovers of their meals neatly clustered on the shore. But the most graphic symbol of the slumbering lake was the carcasses of hundreds of carp, trapped when Moira had drained.

What to me was a thoroughly desolate sight on this eye-squinting autumn day filled State Forests ecologist David Leslie with pleasure. At 1000 ha, Moira Lake is one of the largest lakes on the Murray River floodplain in this neck of the Barmah and Millewa forests, north-east of Echuca, but until two years ago its normal cycle had been reversed. Allowing Moira to dry out was the first stage in an environmental experiment designed to restore some semblance of the natural balance.

Professional fisherman Ron Armstrong scores a callop, or golden perch, in one of his drum nets near Echuca, in central-northern Victoria. Commercial operators like Ron are fighting to keep their licences in the face of tighter controls over the Murray fishery, but it is unlikely that they will be permitted to fish for native fin fish beyond August 2001.

LIFE AND TIMES OF THE MURRAY COD

Murray cod the size of grown men and weighing more than 100 kg have gone down in the annals of Murray River history. Australia's largest freshwater fish is also its most notorious and highly prized.

Anglers still boast of record catches, when the Murray "bubbled with cod", but catching even an average-size fish today is not so easy. Once widespread throughout the Murray–Darling Basin, the Murray cod is now listed as threatened and its populations are "fragmented and patchy". Changes to river flows have largely been blamed for the fish's decline.

Cod are highly territorial and ferocious predators. They begin feeding at 10–14 days of age, when their mouths gape just wide enough to swallow insects, crustaceans, molluscs, and small fish. Later they develop an appetite for larger fish, mussels, yabbies and frogs.

For most of the year cod are sedentary, favouring life in and around logs at the margins of the river channel. But come the breeding season in winter and early spring, when the water temperatures and levels are right, the mature fish become roaming romantics. Radio-tracking has revealed that cod swim upstream to spawn, sometimes swimming up to 120 km, often to the same site.

Females lay up to 60,000 eggs at a time, attaching them to fallen timber for the males to fertilise. It's unproven, but likely that one parent guards the eggs until they hatch two to three weeks later and the larvae drift downstream to establish their own territories.

Researcher John Koehn discovered through radio-tracking that, after spawning, the parents return to the same downstream territory – usually the same snag. Such a homing instinct has not been recorded for any other Australian fish species.

River monster. The giant Murray cod replica at Swan Hill (left) is the closest some anglers get to the real thing (below). A two-year NSW Rivers Survey of the Murray catchment concluded in 1997 that cod populations were "fragmented and patchy and their overall abundance worryingly low". Nearly all the Murray's 36 native fish species have declined in range in the past century; five are now threatened with extinction and a further nine may soon become endangered.

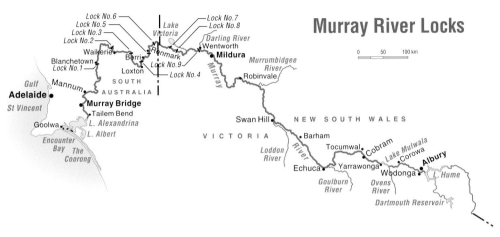

Murray River Locks

0   50   100 km

A carp skeleton and freshwater mussel shells on the scorched bed of 1000 ha Moira Lake suggest grim times but actually bode well for this important wetland in central-southern New South Wales. Drying out the lake by excluding the Murray regulated flows is designed to replicate natural conditions and restore habitat for native fish, birds and plants. "In five years time I hope Moira will be coated in marshwort, ribbonweed and eelweed, swimming with native fish and home to scores of waterbirds," said State Forests ecologist David Leslie, pictured with writer Amanda Burdon.

"Under natural conditions the lake would have been dry for two to four months each summer and autumn for six or seven years in every decade; until last year it was permanently inundated," David explained as we walked further onto the lake, mud crackling underfoot. "This is its second drying in 60 years."

The more natural flow regime at Moira Lake has been achieved through the installation of three regulators, large steel gates positioned at strategic points along the Murray and its tributaries to control the flow of water into its basin. They now exclude water (usually in summer and autumn) to encourage natural drying, or allow water to enter the wetlands (usually in winter and spring) to foster breeding and regeneration.

"When the river levels are high in summer for irrigation, the low-lying areas in the forest and wetlands are usually permanently wet," David said as we dug into the mud for signs of life. "Kept wet, they become unproductive after about five years."

The results, so far, have been encouraging. Terrestrial plants such as joyweed, giant rush, the aromatic black crumbweed and sedges have started to recolonise the lake bed and 10 tonnes of carp have been lost from the lake, hopefully inviting the return of native fish next time it fills. Drying the lake has also aerated the soil, and in the moister patches of mud we found bloodworms, a healthy sign.

But periodic drying is only one side of the coin. Before river management, the Barmah and Millewa forests would have been flooded eight years out of 10, on average; now it's down to four years and the floods rarely linger. David said that just as important as allowing the forests and wetlands to flood now and then was retaining the floodwaters to give plants and animals time to take advantage of the prime conditions.

"Even frogs require a three-month flood to breed properly," he said. "In some years you're almost better off not getting a flood rather than having a short flood that brings the frogs out of dormancy, encourages them to breed and then drops away before they've been successful."

Waterbirds also need consistent water levels to breed effectively, David said. "They're not breeding here yet but the abundance of some species has increased fivefold over the past five years, and if we can get them to feed here regularly, maybe they'll stay."

There was certainly no shortage of waterbirds feeding on the Murray River the following day, when I met wetland ecologist Keith Ward for a boating tour of 29,500 ha Barmah forest. With low river levels exposing the river's muddy flanks, a variety of spindly-legged sentries were out on patrol. Elegant white ibis probed the shallows; intermediate egrets and pied cormorants sat poised on red gum perches overhanging the river, ready to enjoy a

▥ Wetland ecologist Keith Ward surveys plants along a transect line at Hut Lake, in Barmah State Park, north-east of Echuca. In a decade of researching the ecology of the 70,000 ha Barmah and Millewa forests, the largest red-gum forests in Australia, Keith has learnt how plants and animals respond to wetting and drying cycles under the new practices of river regulation. For most semi-permanent wetlands like Hut Lake it has meant a complete reversal of fortunes; shorter, shallower floods now equate to constant low-level flooding, changing the mix of native vegetation markedly.

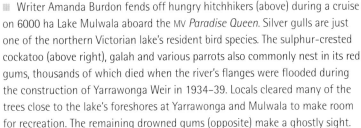

■ Writer Amanda Burdon fends off hungry hitchhikers (above) during a cruise on 6000 ha Lake Mulwala aboard the MV *Paradise Queen*. Silver gulls are just one of the northern Victorian lake's resident bird species. The sulphur-crested cockatoo (above right), galah and various parrots also commonly nest in its red gums, thousands of which died when the river's flanges were flooded during the construction of Yarrawonga Weir in 1934–39. Locals cleared many of the trees close to the lake's foreshores at Yarrawonga and Mulwala to make room for recreation. The remaining drowned gums (opposite) make a ghostly sight.

fish meal; and a single little black cormorant welcomed the sun with glossy outstretched wings. On such a glorious day it was easy to understand why Keith, a wetland ecologist with the Victorian Department of Natural Resources and Environment, counts this stand of majestic giant gums and its wetland counterparts among his favourite places.

"It's a good time for birds; the banks are exposed and there are little fish trapped in diminishing pools," Keith said as we motored slowly along the Murray in the south of the forest. "It's a time of plenty. The forest is one of the biggest ibis staging areas – 12,000 nesting pairs were counted in 1993 during a big, natural flood. Early graziers and field naturalists reported whiskered terns living on lakes of flowering waterlilies, and brolgas as plentiful as sheep in a paddock."

About 120 plant species have been recorded on the Murray's floodplain and 550 in the combined floodplain and forest, which supports 300 vertebrate and innumerable invertebrate species. "The diversity of plants and animals is quite breathtaking," Keith said. "The forest is a hot spot within the Murray system, no question, because you've got broader habitat for a range of species – wetlands for the waterbirds and woodlands for the inland species. The superb parrot is found here and the Barmah and Millewa forests are the only known Murray River breeding locations."

▓ Natural populations of the koala (above) on Ulupna Island, north of Strathmerton, in central-northern Victoria, have been enhanced during the past 25 years by a series of introductions from French and Phillip islands in southern Victoria. Bordered by the Murray and its anabranch Ulupna Creek in the eastern section of Barmah State Park, Ulupna Island is thought to afford the koalas plentiful dining sites and a degree of protection from predators. They are commonly seen high in the branches of red gums, few of which compare with the monster tree dwarfing Strathmerton farmer Geoff Ross-Soden (right) near the junction of Ulupna Creek and the Murray. With an 11 m girth, this old-timer is considered lucky to have survived logging and is rumoured to have served as a landmark for paddle-steamer skippers. Of the 5000 sq. km of red gums along the Murray and its tributaries in NSW and Victoria, almost half are managed as State forest.

Swapping the boat for four wheels, we drove into the wooded south-west of Barmah forest to Steamer Plain, a large clearing where shimmering grasses waved. It was hard to visualise floodwaters lapping this expanse, grazed as it was by emus and kangaroos.

"With the floods, milfoils and Moira grasses grow up through the water column, gudgeons and rainbowfish breed prolifically and the gums hurriedly take on new growth," Keith said of the flood metamorphosis.

"Everything is breeding. Dragonflies are hovering everywhere and huge rafts of pelicans and cormorants fly in to feed on the fish. During major floods we have all the regulators fully open and all the waters converge on the plains. You see fish swimming through the emerging water plants; it must be like one big undersea garden. You put your nets down and catch water scorpions, large diving beetles, tadpoles, juvenile fish and damsel and dragonfly larvae. It's amazing."

A little black cormorant, an intermediate egret, a pied cormorant and a trio of little black cormorants scan the Murray River for food from a handy perch in Barmah forest, in northern Victoria. This forest is a vital breeding site for egrets, cormorants, ibises and herons but previously supported much larger colonies. As with many waterbirds, their breeding is triggered by wetland flooding, ideally in early spring, which stimulates the growth of the plants and animals on which they feed. But river regulation has altered the timing, duration and depth of flooding, diminishing food supplies. Some waterbirds no longer breed here; others tend their nests only while floodwater remains high and abandon their eggs when the level falls.

Red gums shed their bark (above) beside the Murray River at Yarrawonga, in northern Victoria. The river's enduring icon typically grows in single lines on either side of the river, though in regions subject to flooding it sometimes forms forests more than 20 km wide. It is Australia's most widely distributed eucalypt species and one of the few that can survive periodic inundation, growing best when flooded annually in winter. Some trees along the Murray are 500 years old and up to 50 m tall. The western grey kangaroo (right), another native of the Murray Valley, usually prefers box woodlands to the red-gum-lined riverfront. But on 40 sq. km Katarapko Island, in SA's Murray River NP, where this one was photographed, it has a range of habitats to choose from, including grasslands, stands of lignum, woodlands and sandhills. It shares this isolated home with the brushtail possum, water rat, red kangaroo and a small colony of brush-tailed bettongs reintroduced after effective fox and rabbit control programs.

Moonlight mayhem in the mallee

The beep, beep, beep of the radio transmitter intensified as Lin Pope motioned towards a mallee log on the ground before us. We'd spent 30 minutes tracking a radio-collared creature I'd previously known only from photographs. Lin had let me listen to the radio through the headphones as we approached the log.

The sun was high in the sky, casting mottled shadows under the grey-green bush. Reaching inside the log, Lin gently retrieved a finely muscular, beautifully striped creature not much larger than a small squirrel – a numbat named Loretta. Lin checked the animal's overall condition and, careful to avoid the sharp claws, noted her swollen nipples.

"She'll be a mother in a week or 10 days," Lin said. "Numbats generally mate at Christmas and have a 14-day gestation period, so they have their young, usually four, during the last two weeks in January. When they're born, the little numbats are the size of grains of rice. She'll carry them until July, when she leaves them in a burrow while she feeds. In October–November she moves them to a tree and they become independent six weeks later."

Lin added: "You should count yourself lucky. It's not like a zoo here, with animals boxed up in cages. I can never guarantee people will see a numbat."

▥ A suite of magical mallee creatures, including the bilby (left), have been reintroduced to their native habitat within the protective confines of the Yookamurra Sanctuary, north-west of Swan Reach, in SA. By excluding foxes and feral cats, sanctuary staff have also been successful in breeding the greater stick-nest rat (below) and the burrowing bettong, or boodie (bottom), one of Australia's rarest macropods, which had been absent from the region for 80 years. The 3645 ha property is considered the last block of its kind in the State, containing equal thirds of old-growth mallee, sugarwood woodland and whipstick, all of which have been extensively cleared elsewhere.

■ Alert and finely muscled, the numbat is one of eight endangered animals and a host of more common species that have found refuge in Yookamurra Sanctuary. From 15 originally relocated from WA, Yookamurra's numbats have grown to about 150. A fussy eater and highly territorial, the numbat also has precise habitat needs. To support its daily intake of 15,000 termites, it requires mallee old and decayed enough to sustain large termite colonies. Before European settlement, when mallee covered one-fifth of the Australian continent, this did not pose a problem, but wide-scale clearing robbed the numbat of most of its territory. It was Yookamurra's scrubby character and distance from the Murray (10 km) that saved its mallee: it was considered too dense to clear for agriculture and too far from the river to allow the cut timber to be transported for use as paddle-steamer fuel.

Chuffed with myself as much as with the success of the innovative conservation strategy that benefits Loretta, I watched as Lin released the numbat back into the bush. She bounded off like a wave through the mallee undergrowth.

I had joined Lin to experience the wonders of Yookamurra Sanctuary, a 3645 ha property 20 km north-west of the riverfront town of Swan Reach, in southern SA. Managed by Earth Sanctuaries Limited, the pioneering conservation group founded by John Wamsley to provide refuge for many species of Australia's endangered wildlife, Yookamurra is prized for its 1000-year-old mallee trees. It contains about 100,000 of the oldest left on the Australian continent. Almost 1200 ha of the land currently protected within Yookamurra's 14 km vermin-proof fence comprises equal thirds of old-growth mallee, sugarwood woodland, and whipstick, most of which survive only in tiny pockets elsewhere as a result of widespread clearing for farming.

John Wamsley spent six months searching for enough old-growth mallee to support a suite of creatures that once lived here near the Murray, including the bilby, numbat, greater stick-nest rat, burrowing bettong (boodie), brush-tailed bettong (woylie) and plains mouse. The needs of the numbat, lost from SA 90 years ago, were hardest to satisfy. It depends on mallee old and decayed enough to support termites, which it licks up at the rate of 15,000 a day.

"In 1993 we started with 15 numbats," said Lin, Yookamurra's assistant manager. "All are collared, so we can keep an eye on them, and now we have 120–150. We expect it will be another 300 years before the State's remaining mallee will be old enough to support more numbats."

The previous night I'd been introduced to some of Yookamurra's other special residents during a walk with Lin and manager David Hill. Within the safety of the sanctuary's first enclosure, secretive creatures bounded, skipped and loped out of the darkness and into our torchlight to feed on offerings of vegetables and fruit. Plump and rotund, with sweet furred faces, the boodies were the first to emerge, hissing at each other in defence of their food. Then appeared the sprightly and more skittish woylies, among the rarest of Australian macropods and our smallest kangaroo.

But for me the highlight of the evening occurred in an inner enclosure when one of Yookamurra's 28 ungainly bilbies scuttled between my legs, it's bristly grey fur brushing my ankles. Sharp of snout and broad of ear, sporting a white collar and tail tip, the bilbies lolloped in like characters from a children's storybook and champed audibly on the fruit with their small, sharp teeth. Ragged-looking Mr Burns, originally from the Northern Territory and one of the population's patriarchs, squatted politely alongside handsome twins born a little over a year ago.

"It really is easy; you give them the habitat they want and they breed," Lin said. "They surprise you every week. It took me two years to take my first holiday. I was born and bred in the mallee and I've never loved a job so much in my life."

BOOKMARK BIOSPHERE RESERVE

Property boundaries are no barrier to environmental efforts in the Riverland district of SA, where 30 landholders are united under the umbrella of the Bookmark Biosphere Reserve (BBR).

The BBR is one of 330 biosphere reserves established by the United Nations Educational, Scientific and Cultural Organisation (UNESCO) to protect important ecological regions around the world. In Bookmark it's the floodplain wetlands fringing the Murray River and its outlying remnant mallee that are valued.

The BBR covers 9000 sq. km, but from its headquarters on the former Calperum station, north of Renmark, the group's message of economically sustainable conservation is being spread beyond the boundaries of the reserve in the Murray River catchment.

BBR partners include the managers of national parks, game and forestry reserves, government lands and private properties.

The aim of the BBR is to help find cooperative solutions to environmental challenges such as poor water quality, land degradation and loss of wildlife. What makes the approach distinctive, however, is that it doesn't deny the landholders opportunities to make a living.

"Bookmark relies on the community to serve as stewards and undertake responsibility for sustainable management of the natural resources on which their regional lifestyles depend," said Mike Harper, Bookmark Biosphere Trust executive officer.

Research and education is an integral part of the BBR philosophy, and rather than locking up their land, owners are encouraged to share their environmental achievements by serving as guides. Teams of researchers and community groups are currently working on scores of projects – from sustainable citrus industry practices and the protection of black-eared miners to carp exclusion, the development of walking tracks and canoeing reaches and the establishment of native-plant nurseries.

The Lines family of Cobdogla enjoys a quiet paddle on Nockburra Creek, in the SA Riverland's Loch Luna Game Reserve. Encouraging recreation in regions undergoing environmental restoration is one of the tenets of the Bookmark Biosphere Reserve, which brings together 20 landholders across 9000 sq. km in an effort to integrate sustainability and conservation.

BORN IN THE WILDERNESS
From the headwaters to Albury

Fingers of soft afternoon light reached into the snow-gum forest and painted the trees a ghostly white as I entered the remote gully in the foothills of the Australian Alps. Summer had come to the high country. The mountains had all but thrown off their mantles of snow and the snow gums were shedding their mottled skins. My every footfall was cushioned by a moist mattress of springy mosses. The fragrance of native mint hung in the air, but coolness lingered here, too, in the lee of the small rise known as Forest Hill, and I pulled my down vest close to my chest.

It would have been considerably hotter and more intimidating, I reflected, when surveyor Alexander Black passed through here with his party in early 1870. The governments of the day had decided the border between NSW and Victoria would run in an arrow-straight line from Cape Howe, on the south-eastern coast, to the nearest source of the Murray and thence follow the river to the SA border. It was up to Black and his team, carrying heavy measuring chains through the virgin forest, to pinpoint the easternmost origins of the river; it was their calculations, now inscribed forever on maps, that showed our contemporary party the way almost 130 years later.

"Just keep heading to the north-east," instructed Kosciuszko National Park ranger Craig Smith, whom Bill and I had enlisted to guide us to the cradle of the Murray in the heart of The Pilot Wilderness, 60 km as the crow flies south-west of Jindabyne. Having made camp at Cowombat Flat, a clearing west of Forest Hill, which abuts the State border, we'd set off on foot with contour maps and a compass, determined to reach the source before sundown.

At this point the Murray was just a small brook. It was relatively simple to follow it upstream, fringed as it was by tall, feathery mountain tea-tree, but the search intensified when it disappeared into a series of sphagnum soaks. At one, we startled a grey brumby drinking; it turned on its hooves and vanished into the bush like a shadow. Further uphill the soaks converged on a damp glade strewn with fallen trees and spidery lichens.

"I reckon this is close to the source," Craig said confidently, squatting in the sodden marsh, one foot in NSW and the other in Victoria. "This is where the water that flows off The Pilot collects and comes to the surface." Our expedition was hardly on the scale of Black's, which

▓ Writer Amanda Burdon and Kosciuszko NP ranger Craig Smith (opposite) savour the view while climbing The Pilot (1830 m), the Murray's watershed in the Australian Alps. Water from rain and melting snow runs off the east side of Pilot Mountain to the Ingeegoodbee and the Snowy River. On the west it runs to Pilot Creek and the Murray. At Cowombat Flat, the clearing on the right, the Murray tumbles out of the woodland on its way through Kosciuszko NP.

■ Australia's most significant river begins life in a timbered sphagnum bog (below), near the base of Forest Hill, in the heart of The Pilot Wilderness near its border with Alpine NP. Underground springs form three marshy soaks in a snow-gum forest clearing (right), where Amanda Burdon and ranger Craig Smith explore the vivid alpine grasslands. The Murray's catchment above Hume Dam represents just 2 per cent of the Murray–Darling Basin's total area but contributes almost 40 per cent of the river's flow.

took 11 months to travel 64 km south-west from the source, but I was delighted with our discovery all the same. We were on top of Australia, at the birthplace of its greatest river, and my own Murray River journey had truly begun.

From this boggy snowgrass meadow, I traced the infant Murray back downstream. I saw it tumble over rocks and among bossiaea and hakea bushes. Growing bigger and stronger, it tickled tussock grasses and danced among tea-tree on Cowombat Flat before running away to the Murray Valley.

We had a clear view of its route the next day, the first of summer. Craig led Bill and me on another pilgrimage, a steep, hour-long climb to the top of The Pilot (1830 m), due north of Forest Hill. Water from rain and melting snow spills off The Pilot's granite flanks, leaches underground and seeps out at the foot of Forest Hill. So, atop The Pilot we were, theoretically, at the Murray's loftiest beginnings. Far below, the crumpled mountain range parted to provide passage for its child.

From The Pilot's foothills the Murray winds for almost 50 km between the wilderness of the Kosciuszko and Alpine national parks – the preserve of skiers, bushwalkers and dedicated anglers – before making its public debut at Tom Groggin station. At this historic property, visitors not fortunate enough to have a ranger guide or not inclined to backpack (no vehicles are permitted in The Pilot Wilderness) can catch their first glimpse of the spirited Murray as it plummets into the Biggara Valley.

Dust hung over the station when Bill and I, having followed Davies Plain Track from The Pilot, emerged into the picturesque valley, its encircling mountains blue in the evening light. Managers Linda and Trevor Davis and owner Duncan McDonald were winding up a tiring day of cattle drafting. Bellowing Hereford and angus drowned out our introductions. Many of the beasts were destined for the saleyards, but a select few had been chosen to spend the summer grazing on the rich high-country pastures.

Later, as he relaxed over a cold beer, straight-talking Trevor sought to explain his affection for the riverfront property.

"I first came to Tom Groggin when I was 14 and did a bit of cattle work for about a year. I'm pretty proud to be back here managing the place," he said. "It's a job, but it's a great job to have. Why would you want to live anywhere else? It's surrounded by national park, we're at the foot of the Murray River and the tradition and heritage of this place are very important."

The history is woven around the larger-than-life character of Jack Riley, a former Tom Groggin station manager and, as legend has it, the person on whom Banjo Paterson modelled the hero of his poem *The Man from Snowy River*. A legendary horseman, Jack used to catch and break the brumbies that roamed the surrounding hills. He is said to have shared tales of his daring escapades with Paterson during an evening in 1890, a short time before the much-loved ballad was published in *The Bulletin*.

Kosciuszko NP ranger Craig Smith clambers through a thicket of mountain tea-tree (above left) to glimpse the juvenile Murray at its source. It eventually spills out onto Cowombat Flat (above), fringed by small-fruited hakea bushes. A catchment's elevation dictates a river's energy, and the Murray's catchment is low by world standards for a watercourse of its length.

Saddled up for a 10-day outing from Khancoban to the Snowy River, riders take advantage of the shallow water to cross the Murray in the Alpine NP. "It's the Man from Snowy River legend and the mountain scenery that attract most of our guests," said tour leader John Williams, who has been leading groups through the mountains for more than 12 years. Even away from the alps, the views are just as breathtakingly beautiful, as this view (opposite) south-eastwards from Towong towards the Snowy Mountains shows.

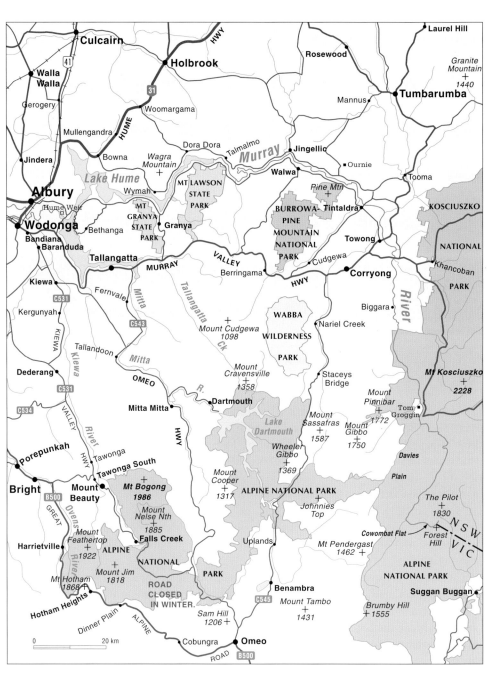

Shrouded in dust, Linda Davis (above) drafts Herefords at Tom Groggin station in readiness for the annual summer cattle drive into the Snowy Mountains. Linda and husband Trevor manage the 810 ha property, where the Murray emerges from Kosciuszko NP. Trevor lived in this simple log hut (opposite) as a teenager during his first stint at the station. "I stayed for about 12 months and it was always my dream to come back and run this place," he said. "Tom Groggin is one of a kind and we're still working it like they did 50 years ago."

"Many people come here thinking they might see the mystical Jack Riley riding about," said Trevor, Jack's modern-day incarnation. "Or they ask to meet Tom Groggin himself." Tourists are common in the warmer months but winter tests even hardy blokes like Trevor. "We get good rainfall here, more than anywhere else, but the climate is cooler, too," he said. "It gets bloody cold. The wind and rain nearly cut you in half and we usually get snow at least once a year."

At that time of year the Murray's cradle is frequented only by skiers and back-country enthusiasts, but come spring the animated river lures another breed – daredevil rafters and paddlers. I was glad of the warm weather when I joined a group about to launch six rafts 5 km north-west of Tom Groggin station.

"During the snow melt it's like being on a roller-coaster ride," said my whitewater guide, Boris Everson, who spends the September–February season taking willing paddlers on the ride of their lives. "It's a very challenging river, especially when it starts to drop. It becomes very technical for the guides as rocks appear and the paths are not so defined. You need to be able to read the river and react to it. Up here, the Murray's flow is completely natural."

Fast reactions were certainly obligatory as we paddled 16 km downstream, bobbing and banking over boulders through Murray Gates, a narrow granite chute shaded by candlebark and blue gum, silver wattle and peppermint. Gentle ripples in the first reach gave Bill, Ross, our fellow paddler, and me time to test our technique before our raft was sucked into a corrugated stretch of rapids and we were propelled violently downstream. Paddling forward, then backwards, hard right, then hard left and sometimes simply holding on for dear life, we responded promptly to bronzed Boris's every direction, the river's boisterous heartbeat throbbing beneath us.

"Many people don't know of the upper Murray as a whitewater rafting venue, so it's remained a well-kept secret," Boris yelled as we bounced off yet another hidden obstacle, his face breaking into a mischievous smile. "You gotta love it." And we did, emerging jelly-legged but joyous at Bunroy Creek junction at the end of the day.

Scrambling up the riverbank to catch our bus north to Khancoban, I noticed a ramshackle house growing out of the hillside, partly hidden by fruit trees and tangled plants. A few days later I had the pleasure of meeting its occupant, Frank Thompson, a gentle soul perfectly at home in this wild and secluded place. At 88, Frank is a little unsteady on his feet and his skin has developed the papery texture of old age, but he leads a fiercely independent life in his "bachelor quarters", the 6 ha property he calls *Little Niche*. He's not short of company, with his 14 free-ranging chooks, two sheep and three dogs, and he welcomes the occasional visit from family, friends and fishermen.

Frank paid for his one-third share of the property by selling fox skins, before buying out his fellow shareholders and moving in himself in 1981. "I slept under a sheet of iron leaning up against a tree at first," he said with a toothless smile. "I did improve my sleeping quarters eventually. I got three or four more pieces of iron to keep myself dry."

■ Whitewater rafters shoot the Murray Gates, a narrow granite channel between Tom Groggin station and Bunroy Creek, in the Murray's headwaters. Though rambunctious at its source, the Murray soon settles into such a sedate pace that it is surprising it lasts the distance to SA. Run-off in the catchment is low, the river's gradient is slight and for much of its circuitous journey it traverses semi-arid country, receiving little sustenance from major tributaries.

In the cluttered kitchen of the house he built, Frank cleared away newspapers and tucker from the table and, over afternoon tea, told us about his simple routine. He still enjoys a spot of trout fishing and gold prospecting in the Murray, and he drives to Corryong, about 40 km away, once a week to collect his mail and shoppping, but it's the solitude he relishes.

"They call me a hermit, but I'm just living my life and enjoying it," he said. "I'm a bit of a rogue, and when I came here I thought nobody would find me. I love this place in the bush and I'll probably die here. I think it's the best spot in Victoria, possibly Australia. There's national park all around, and the river. There's nobody above me and Tom Groggin station on the Murray."

A lifeline emerges

Leaving Frank in his splendid isolation, Bill and I drove on through the rich, rolling pastures of the Biggara Valley, where the large black-and-white Holstein milking cows easily outnumber the residents. Beyond the tiny settlement of Towong, we headed for Tintaldra, a larger township on the lush Murray River flats. The evening patrons, as dusty-looking as they were dry-throated, were already gathering at the Tintaldra Hotel when we arrived. The first pub on the river, about 170 km east of Albury, it was built in 1870 a stone's throw from the lazy watercourse that underpins the local economy. It is now run by Maija and Alf Wilson.

A small clearing in the woodland and a scattering of buildings (below left) reveal the presence of *Little Niche*, the home of contented bachelor Frank Thompson (below) at the junction of Little Bunroy Creek and the Murray. "I enjoy company but up here I can be myself, no worries," said the independent 88-year-old. "I don't know what loneliness is."

■ Time-honoured traditions are still observed at Tintaldra, the first European settlement on the upper Murray, 170 km east of Albury. The old wood-fired oven at the back of the Tintaldra General Store no longer works but store-keeper Betty Walton (above) is only too pleased to cook up a storm for visitors, and backyard cricket (above right) remains the order of the day on summer afternoons. Sited at an important river crossing, the town still boasts a store-cum-post office and a hotel (opposite top), but the police station has closed and the customs house (opposite bottom) was moved to nearby Tintaldra station, home of fourth-generation Mackinnons Henry, Harriet, Edwina and Amelia.

Founded in the late 1830s, Tintaldra was the first European settlement on the upper Murray. A township comprising a post office, police station, general store and customs house soon sprouted to support the district's only punt crossing, and before long Tintaldra was a thriving business centre catering for surrounding farming families.

"There used to be an accordion band here and a dance every Saturday," said Maija, a former opera singer, as we chatted on the pub's cool veranda. "There was a tennis club, cricket club, football club and golf club. Of course now, the way the rural industry is going, no-one has time. Big properties and big responsibilities." Although now a quieter place, Tintaldra has a golf club and a well-respected pony club.

A stalwart of the small community, Maija is president of the governing committee that manages the township's recreation reserve. She serves as a volunteer for the visitor centre and museum, would dearly love to re-establish the drama group and has "inherited" the church choir at nearby Corryong.

"Running the pub you don't just sell grog; you're part of the community," she said. "During floods I answer the phone with: 'River Advisory Service'. Tintaldra is the best-kept secret in Victoria. People don't know they're coming here and half the time they don't know where they are when they get here."

The keeper of Tintaldra's historic general store and all its treasured stories is Betty Walton. She shared her passion for the Murray with me over tea and scones in the timber building that has changed little since 1864. A bush poet, tourism advocate and amateur historian, she swapped the unforgiving Cronulla surf in Sydney's south for the river's grassy banks 25 years ago.

"The river's the region's lifeblood but I think many people have to learn that it doesn't belong to them; it belongs to everyone," she said. "We are the beginning up here, and what we do is reflected downstream. To me the river's got that prehistoric character, like it's been here for millions and millions of years, and of course it has."

The ancient charm of the Murray was brought strikingly into focus when Bill and I took to the skies with pilot Glenn Wilson in a light aircraft above Corryong and tracked the Murray from its source to Lake Hume. As it flowed north of Forest Hill, it zigzagged though the pleated, timber-clad mountains and spilled out into the verdant Biggara Valley, a patchwork of green pastures and brown stubble textured wart-like with hay bales.

Though it was hidden from my view, I knew it was here that the Snowy Mountains Hydro-electric Scheme directs the waters of the Snowy and Eucumbene rivers through two tunnels under the Great Divide to the Murray and the Murrumbidgee rivers. The Snowy's waters, captured at Island Bend, are diverted either by tunnel to Lake Eucumbene for storage or transferred directly west through a second tunnel to Geehi Reservoir, on the western side of the ranges. From there, the water passes through two power stations, Murray 1 and Murray 2, before being released into the Murray via one of its tributaries, the Swampy Plain River, at Khancoban.

Escaping from the mountains to the plains, the Murray winds through the dreamy Upper Towong landscape before swallowing the Swampy Plain River just downstream of the township. Having cooled its heels in billabongs and anabranches that we could see winking like quicksilver, it curls past the townships of Tintaldra, Walwa and Jingellic. More reluctant now, as though anticipating its fate, it disperses into a tangle of wetlands, many rendered jade with duckweed, west of Talmalmo, before acquiescing to the insistent grip of Lake Hume's northern arm.

Down on the ground, Bill and I drove 60 km north-west from Tintaldra to meet a couple who will leave their mark on this magical landscape. Bill and Judy Wells, committed members of the Murray Catchment Management Committee (MCMC) and the Upper Murray Catchment Network (UMCN), had lunch waiting for us at 390 ha Ournie station, where they run 200 Hereford breeders and 1200 merino sheep. The farm's annual fortunes were being told that day, with the much-anticipated visits of wool- and cattle-buyers, but Bill would not be distracted from his environmental message.

"I feel very deeply about passing on high-quality Murray River water," Bill said over our more-than-generous meal. "It's almost spiritual; we feel that the land has to be respected. In important catchments like this, we are only caretakers. If we stuff it up here, the river's gone. Man, in his impudence, believes he can tame a river, and perhaps he can for a while, but not forever."

Sunset paints the still river in soft hues as trout fishing guide Ron Vise (right) makes another cast on the evening rise near his upper Murray home at Towong. "Spring to autumn is the best time for trout fishing, when you get the mayflies hatching and nymphs emerging," said Ron. "The cooler the water, the more activity generally, but it's just nice to be on the river when the light's right." Downstream at Albury's Hume Weir Trout Farm, one of the 4000 glistening brood rainbow trout (below) testifies to the health of captive fish stocks. The hatchery, which produces about 70 tonnes of trout annually for Sydney, Canberra and local restaurants, relies on the Murray to fill its 1.5 ha of ponds before returning the water to the river via a natural wetland. While fishing remains one of the most popular river pastimes, it is rivalled near Walwa by canoeing in the broad, safe reaches. Here, Albury duo Rachael Crane and Jenni Hayes (opposite) were given a welcome tow after experiencing a minor mishap.

In his role as a member of the MCMC, Bill has worked hard toward achieving the committee's ambition of "a diverse and healthy catchment for all generations" in 12,150 ha of the Ournie catchment region. And where better to start than in your own backyard? When Bill and Judy bought the property 23 years ago, Ournie Creek, which enters the Murray on their land, was badly eroded by cattle and polluted by farm run-off. Its restoration became their priority and I saw the success of their measures after lunch as we wandered along the creek's shady banks.

"We've wound the creek back into its old course, stabilised the banks with rocks, fenced it off and planted native trees," Bill said. "The water quality is now quite good; trees planted by other property owners in the creek's upper reaches are taking up the phosphorus and chemical residues and we'll soon be installing key monitoring points to check the creek's content before it enters the Murray."

But the dedication of the UMCN and Bill and Judy to their river environment isn't limited to Ournie Creek. Members are also planting trees on road verges to create wildlife corridors that link nearby national parks, reserves and wooded private properties; they monitor bores and wells for signs of salinisation; and they are planning to fence off some riverside areas from stock to allow vegetation to regenerate. Azure kingfishers and rainbow bee-eaters have returned to Ournie station, and Bill and Judy hope water rats, platypus and koalas will soon follow.

■ Come the cod-fishing season, Joy and Barry Wilson (above) pack their rods and swap their Corryong home for their camp at the Walwa Caravan Park. A Murray angler for 60 years, Barry has made the annual pilgrimage since 1966. Upstream, grazier and conservationist Bill Wells (above right) has little time for fishing. His priority as owner of Ournie station, 18 km north-west of Tintaldra, is to implement sustainable farming practices – such as tree planting, stock exclusions and bank erosion remedies – to safeguard the river's health. Glinting in a patchwork of paddocks between Biggara and Towong Upper in the upper Murray Valley (opposite), the river's meanders and billabongs sustain farms that produce anything from canola to milk.

Lazy days on the river

The Murray River winds its way into the hearts and minds of Australians right along its circuitous length. Some see it simply as an economic necessity, others as a balm that soothes their tired souls. Retiree Barry Wilson is one of the latter.

When we met in the shade of the cottonbush elms at the Walwa Caravan Park, he was preparing for a night's cod-fishing by the light of the full moon (because he reckons they're easier to catch then). The cod season had opened only two days earlier, but he'd already landed a 3.6 kg fish and was confident of bigger things to come. Large white Y-fronts and navy blue worker's singlets strung out on the guide ropes to dry marked the well-equipped tent that Barry and his wife Joy occupy for three months over the summer break, just two hours drive from their Corryong home.

"We usually arrive about Christmas time and fish till it gets too cold or we get sick of the caretaker or the fish run out," Barry, 66, said of the ritual they've observed since 1966. He grew up on the Murray and has been wetting lines in its waters for more than 60 years.

"It's not a bad spot; it's a beautiful river," he added. "The fish are a bit harder to find these days but there's still a few about. I know where the cod are, but you can't make them bite. There have been fish I've tried to catch for years; I've got names for some of them."

Continuing our downstream journey, to where the river loiters in wide, sensual bends, I remembered the words of poet Graeme Kinross Smith, who wrote that the Murray "... is always changing within its essential changelessness. It is always a river, but never the same river in place or time... You must smell the Murray, taste it, listen to it. And soon you find that you want to read its changing face wherever you can reach it, and the river is in your soul."

The profound influence that the Murray has had on artist Jill Raymond is reflected in the vibrant creations I saw several days later in her riverfront studio just upstream of Talmalmo. The Murray is languid here as it approaches Lake Hume and, overlooking a glimmering sweep of water, Jill is well positioned to record in colourful detail the narrative of her river life. Her ceramics, collages and artwork swirl with river scenes and characters. Jill and husband Geoff were living in Adelaide but, having both been born on the Murray at Mildura, were keen to return to the river. They found this haven east of Albury four years ago.

"Our life is idyllic, our stress levels zero and it's a stimulating place for me as an artist," Jill said as she showed me some of her favourite pieces. "I get up every day and see an explosion of colour. Some days it makes me feel giddy. The river and the stories behind the people and their lives are my big inspiration. Something draws you back to the river time and time again. I'm not quite sure what it is. I only know that when I'm away from it for long periods I feel a great sense of dislocation."

For a more pragmatic perspective on the Murray, I visited Jill and Geoff's neighbours, the Smithwicks, a few kilometres down the road. Their 1000 ha cattle and sheep property, currently supporting about 1300 head of angus and Herefords, has been in the family since 1866 and is almost fully enclosed by a horseshoe bend in the river. Smithwick patriarch and third-generation landholder, 84-year-old Bob, was born 13 km upstream and has had little cause to stray far. As we inspected aerial photographs he and his son Vyner use to plan river-erosion remedies and tree plantings, Bob told me his forebears were not nearly as far-sighted.

"When my family arrived here it was all lagoons along the foot of the hills," said Bob, appropriately shod in gumboots. "They dug 24 miles [39 km] of drains by hand, and in those days trees were public enemy number one. My uncle's philosophy was that when he had to buy every stick of wood he needed, he'd be happy, so he rung every tree on the place. Now we're planting as fast as we can, about 3000 river red gums, silver wattles and river bottlebrush this year. The river's our lifeblood. We've only got about two miles [5 km] of boundary fence; all the rest – about nine miles [14 km] – is river. It's cheap fencing."

Later, in the shade of the errant willows that now fringe large stretches of the Murray, Vyner explained the family's farming philosophy. "We aim to look after the land first and provide pastures for our grazing stock second, and that's what you make a living from," he said. "Most of Australia gets along quite well without a river, but we've had it all our lives. We drink from it and swim in it. It's vital in drought times; if a dam dries up, we open a gate

■ Art has imitated life for Jill Raymond (right) - seen here with some of her distinctive ceramic work - ever since she moved to Talmalmo from Adelaide four years ago. The vibrant upper Murray landscape has never failed to provide her with subject matter, inspiring colourful scenes for her work and a peaceful state of mind. Downstream neighbours Vyner and Bronwyn Smithwick (below), of Talmalmo station, have long valued the special qualities of this riverfront haven. "I never get tired of the river or take it for granted; it's just magic," said Vyner, whose family took up the 1000 ha sheep and cattle property in 1866. Just below Talmalmo, the youthful river is embraced by Lake Hume, home of the Wymah Ferry and its past and present operators, Tony Edwards and Lorraine Waite (opposite left), pictured sharing a yarn during the 10-minute crossing. By the time the Murray reaches Albury it is a wide and noble channel (opposite right), plied by the PS *Cumberoona* and frequented by many a river rascal at Noreuil Park.

and let the stock go to the river. In time, stock will be excluded from the river, certainly the sensitive areas. We're trying to fence off the sensitive areas now along our river frontage."

When he was a "little tacker", Vyner and his brother Charlie used to row a boat across the Murray, collect their pushbikes and ride almost 6 km to school. "We spent a lot of time down on the river once we became waterproof," he reminisced.

"When I got older and went out socially to Burrowye or Walwa, I'd row across the river and someone would pick you up on the other side. You'd have a wild night and they'd pour you back into the boat, and if you were lucky you'd get home dry. Not everybody did!"

The individuality of the Murray that sustains the Talmalmo river flats, bubbling over time-worn pebbles on its westward course, is lost just a few kilometres downstream when it enters Lake Hume. Bill and I followed the river's northern bank to Wymah, crossed to Victoria on the ferry and continued via Bethanga to the lake, where yachts danced like butterflies on the cobalt waters.

It was warm by the time we reached Albury, where the Murray, liberated from Lake Hume, greets its first city. There the river drifted casually through Noreuil Park. Swallows performed aerobatics above its eddying surface; fearless boys leapt from the overhanging boughs of red gums; and families picnicked in shaded comfort on the billiard-table lawns. Bill and I needed little encouragement to join them.

THE RIVERINE PLAINS
Albury to Echuca

The grapevines of All Saints Estate were celebrating autumn in grand style, their leaves an earthy palette of orange, vermilion and brown. Until two weeks ago, a fleet of picking machines had been prowling among them, plucking the ripe fruit from the trellises during a frenetic harvest that extends from February to May. But on the day Bill and I visited this, one of the Rutherglen region's oldest vineyards, the picking was over and the mood sedate. The century-old elms that led in a grand avenue to the estate's imposing red-brick castle were dropping their yellow leaves, and pied currawongs called mournfully overhead.

The district's first settlers were more intent on digging up the earth than cultivating it. When George Sutherland-Smith and John Banks propagated the first vines at the All Saints site in 1864, the nearby port of Wahgunyah, on the Murray about 9 km north-west of Rutherglen, was a busy supply depot for the 2000 or so goldminers at Beechworth and Wahgunyah itself.

As I entered the austere All Saints castle to meet sales and marketing manager Kevin Bascomb, I wondered what those diggers, huddled under canvas, would have made of this ostentatious example of Scottish architecture, built in 1873, and its formal rose garden. One Chinese contingent that stayed on after the gold veins were exhausted was warmly welcomed; its members began work pruning and picking in the vineyard, and the corrugated-iron dormitory that housed them is now one of several National Trust buildings in the All Saints complex.

"The estate is steeped in history," said Kevin, pointing to walls bearing international wine prizes dating back to 1873, and a collection of bulbous oak casks crafted in the early 1900s. "Rutherglen is the oldest continuous wine-making region in Victoria. Our reputation was founded on fortified wines, but today they represent only a small proportion of our overall wine sales."

Some 16 wineries straddle the Murray River and Murray Valley Highway around the township of Rutherglen. With 5 km of river frontage, All Saints Estate is one of the largest, its 58 ha of vineyards producing a diverse range of styles. The estate is fortunate to be able to supplement annual rainfall (635 millimetres) with river irrigation, but Kevin said the region owes its wine-making success to the long, dry autumns that allow the grapes to ripen to a high sugar level.

▦ Stately 125-year-old elm trees (opposite) make a grand entrance to All Saints Estate winery at Wahgunyah, among the oldest in the Rutherglen region of northern Victoria. Beyond the avenue is an ornate forecourt garden and imposing brick building modelled on Scotland's Castle of Mey. They are legacies of wine-making pioneers George Sutherland-Smith and John Banks, who planted the first grapevines here in 1864. The pair commonly escorted their produce aboard the paddle-steamer *Eliza Jane* as it travelled down the Murray from Wahgunyah to the Echuca railhead.

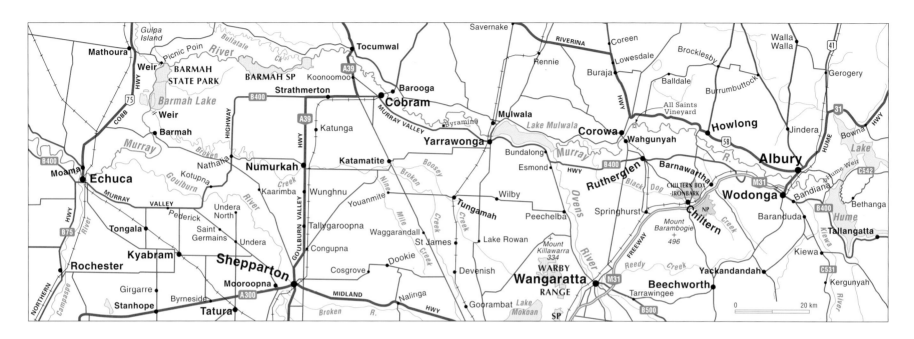

Cameleer Lindsay Chugg leads his charges, Hannah and Tara, bearing riders, from right, Seth Gripe, Rachel Woodmansey and David Willis across Sunday Creek Bridge at Pfeiffers Winery, near Wahgunyah, during one of Linbrae Camel Farm's wine treks. Some 17 wineries straddling the Murray River and Murray Valley Highway cater to tourists visiting the historic township of Rutherglen. Many vignerons rely on the Murray's water to irrigate their vines, which produce robust red, fresh white and rich fortified wines. The availability of irrigation water, abundant sunshine, sandy loam soils and long, dry autumns are the secrets of the region's wine-making success.

With an eye for perfection, cooper Garry McCluskey (left) inspects one of his hand-crafted barrels at the Rutherglen Keg Factory, housed in the original coopers' workshop of the All Saints Estate winery. Fashioned from aged American oak, the barrels come with a 20-year guarantee. Subtleties of blending and cellaring are second nature to third-generation winemaker and renowned Victorian wine judge Bill Chambers (below), who still uses his family's vintage 1-tonne wine press at the rustic Chambers Rosewood Winery nearby.

"With such a long vintage, we have flexibility," he explained. "We can make a sparkling wine or delicate riesling early or leave the grapes on the vine to make a full-bodied chardonnay later. The paddocks yield about 5–7 tonnes per acre [.405 ha]. It's all a product of good soil, sunshine and water."

The heavy reliance on the river of Murray communities came clearly into view as we left Corowa and drove west on the Riverina Highway towards Mulwala. Barely 15 km on, the graceful river began to spread out into a wide blue basin. It was the beginnings of 4450 ha Lake Mulwala, where the Murray is impounded above Yarrawonga Weir for diversion to irrigation areas in NSW's southern Riverina and Victoria's Murray Valley. The victims of this mammoth engineering undertaking were plainly obvious: hundreds of red gums drowned when the lake was formed in 1939. Red gums need to be immersed in water periodically, but only for limited periods. If flooded for too long, they die. Stark, devoid of limbs and leaves, these trees were a tragic presence.

Though intended mainly to ensure an irrigation supply, the lake was quickly adopted for recreation. Mulwala, I observed, was like an Australian coastal town, except we were almost 400 km inland. Watersport clubs offering fishing, skiing, rowing and powerboating flourish on the foreshores, and there's no shortage of motels or holiday lettings to

A blaze of vermilion autumn foliage ignites grapevines growing in the shadow of the landmark castle at All Saints Estate winery, near Rutherglen. The district's first vineyards were planted in the 1850s and were extended by miners who remained after the 1860s gold rushes at nearby Beechworth, Chiltern and Wahgunyah. The young wine industry was almost ruined by an outbreak of the dreaded phylloxera disease in the late 1890s but has bounced back to produce wines now ranked among the world's best.

accommodate the summer hordes that buzz across the shallow waters. Locals boast that the climate shared by Mulwala and her Victorian sister town, Yarrawonga, is better than that of the Gold Coast – a dazzling 2800 hours of sunshine a year. As if it needed more to recommend it, Mulwala is also home to the largest golf course in Australia.

But my first stop was not the lake or the greens but Yarrawonga Weir, where ruddy-faced reservoir controller Colin Fitzpatrick was overseeing maintenance to one of the structure's 10 steel flood gates and winding down a busy spring–summer irrigation period. As we watched the last of the season's allocation trickle into the cavernous rock-lined earth channel known as Yarrawonga Main Channel, Colin told me that during the season up to 3000 megalitres a day can be diverted through it to the Murray valley irrigation district in Victoria.

However, important though this channel is, it is dwarfed by another conduit, the Mulwala Canal, which emerges from the NSW side of the lake, located upstream of the main weir structure where we were standing.

"Up to 10,000 megalitres of water a day flow through the Mulwala Canal to the southern Riverina," Colin said. "This weir and the associated diversion structures are one of the most critical operating points on the river."

Later, as Colin traced the Mulwala Canal on a map, I reflected on the extraordinary life-giving properties of the Murray. Almost 3000 km of capillaries branch off the Mulwala Canal, pumping the "liquid gold" across more than 7500 sq. km. And there are many such capillaries within the Murray's complex circulatory system. Rice growers, beef and wool producers, horticulturists, dairy farmers and cereal croppers in distant spots need only place

A memorable image of symmetry in gold, these plantation poplars between Yarrawonga and Cobram once provided wood for match manufacturer Bryant and May. Now abandoned, they fire the imagination with their burnished autumn finery. Land was first granted in the Cobram region in 1845, for sheep grazing, but wheat cropping and irrigated agriculture were quick to follow suit. Today the Murray flats are largely given over to intensive dairying and stone-fruit, citrus, wine, vegetable and cereal production. Visitors find solitude in the river's secluded sandy beaches and pleasant bushwalking trails.

their orders, a few days in advance in many cases, to have the Murray's riches pumped from storages such as this to their door.

Cruising Lake Mulwala aboard the MV *Paradise Queen*, I saw that foreshore real estate is a luxury afforded many Mulwala and Yarrawonga residents along the lake's 15 km length. Among them are Alan and Laurie Way, who run the popular Shoreline Caravan Park at Mulwala.

Blustery conditions had whipped up whitecaps the next morning when I met the couple for a chat, and only a few hardy anglers were out on the lake. But in the warmth of the park's cramped office, whose walls were decorated with boating signs, advertisements for bardy-grub bait and photographs of anglers hoisting aloft massive fish, Alan told me the lake is cluttered with boats during the Easter and Christmas holidays.

About 30,000 people descend on Mulwala and Yarrawonga each year, many of them intent on realising a dream. "The lake is one of the country's premier Murray cod fisheries," Alan said. "People come here for the mythical cod. They know they won't catch as big a fish as in the olden days, but there are more cod in this system now than 15 years ago because of new size limits and fishing rules, so your chances of catching one are pretty good."

A parade (opposite) clogs Belmore Street, Yarrawonga's main thoroughfare, during the annual Murray Muster and 1999 Australian Bush Poetry Championships. The four-day event attracts healthy crowds and almost 200 performers from all over Australia to celebrate our nation's folklore and bush verse. Among the more colourful entertainers was Wangaratta poet and Australian whip-cracking champion Noel Cutler (above), who amused patrons of Old's Bakery with his eloquence and antics.

The pace is fast and furious as competitors in the mixed K1 division (left) set off on the third day of the Red Cross Murray Marathon in the Barmah forest, near Echuca, in northern Victoria. The 404 km race attracts up to 1000 competitors in 90 divisions and 4000–5000 officials and land support crew every year. Paddlers complete five legs of roughly 90 km in five days of racing from Yarrawonga to Swan Hill immediately after Christmas. The race culminates in an enormous New Year's Eve celebration. During its 31-year history the marathon has raised almost $2 million for the Victoria branch of Australian Red Cross.

An angler and his companion try their luck on 4450 ha Lake Mulwala (above), the artificial water body formed in 1939 by the building of Yarrawonga Weir (right), between Yarrawonga and Mulwala. The lake was quickly adopted for recreation, though its prime function is to provide a permanent irrigation pool for the southern Riverina in NSW and Victoria's Murray Valley Irrigation Area. "The concrete wall raised the river level upstream by 8 m and allowed channels to be dug on either side to gravity-feed farms," said reservoir controller Colin Fitzpatrick. "We send water to irrigators according to their requirements." Up to 13,000 megalitres a day are diverted from the weir through the two lengthy irrigation channels. The 2880 km Mulwala Canal supplies rice, dairy pastures, cereal, beef and sheep farmers over 7500 sq. km, and the 957 km Yarrawonga Main Channel waters dairy pastures, orchards and beef and sheep properties across 1280 sq. km. Curiously, the lake was never officially opened because of the outbreak of World War II; instead an official ceremony was held on its 50th anniversary.

A palace fit for a Hume

Elizabeth Hume was still mourning her husband John, shot by bushrangers at Gunning, in south-eastern NSW, when she and her nine children arrived on the banks of the Murray River in 1842. Her brother-in-law, explorer Hamilton Hume, had passed through the region west of present-day Yarrawonga 18 years previously during his 1824 explorations with William Hovell and recalled the promising soil and river outlook. When his brother died, he claimed a 34,425 ha cattle run on Elizabeth's behalf, installed her there with her family and set about supervising the construction of Byramine Homestead.

It was a fine site for a house, I reckoned, as Bill and I approached the whitewashed homestead 15 km west of Yarrawonga. Perched on a sandy knoll, it faced the river and enjoyed its cooling breezes, yet was safe from floods and had a reliable well. What in Elizabeth's day would have been riverflat pastures are now a vast market garden, decorated with thriving vegetables, but her home and its 5 ha surrounds remain almost as she left them.

Byramine Homestead is now listed by the National Trust and owned by the Ferguson family, and it was clear from the moment we met that bubbly Lynne Ferguson takes great pride in its history.

"When the property was sold in the 1880s it was the largest subdivision on record in Victoria," she said. "But the history of the building was not known until 1964, when a local historian unearthed its details. When we took over two years ago, dust had collected in the ceilings and you couldn't get through some doors for the cobwebs. It was sagging and abandoned."

Now fully restored, with just the original shingle roof sacrificed for galvanised iron, the Murray pine-and-brick building is open to the public and as a venue for special functions. Thoughtfully designed by an English architect, it is hexagonal in shape to allow Elizabeth to see in every direction, and it features an unusual octagonal inner "fortress-room".

"She was paranoid about another attack and had nine children to defend," Lynne said during my private tour. "As far as pioneer homes went, this must have been something of a palace – four bedrooms, a dining room, parlour, entry hall, meat-hanging room and butler's parlour. For it to have been built in one fell swoop is amazing."

Hamilton Hume remained with his sister-in-law for a year before leaving her to manage the property alone. I could not imagine the challenges that Elizabeth must have faced as she struggled to raise her large family in such isolation. One daughter drowned in a nearby lagoon and Elizabeth suffered bronchial ailments throughout her life, finally succumbing to measles in her 60s. The face, framed by a high-necked lace blouse, that stared down from a photograph on the fortress-room wall was stern, and wore the weariness born of hardship.

"They arrived with only what they could bring from Gunning; Elizabeth had the clothes she was wearing, some materials to build the house and several tree saplings to plant in memory of her late husband," Lynne said, pointing to the mature elms and kurrajongs that now shade most of the front garden.

A penchant for horsing around is just one of the eccentricities of wiry Barmah "bushranger" Graeme Padgett, better known as Padge, who, with his partner Debbie Jackson, leads riding tours in Barmah State Park, near Strathmerton. A former shearer, builder and truck driver, Padge started offering weekend rides along the Murray's banks almost 15 years ago and now shares his passion with up to 1500 riders annually. Living in a two-room hut that lacks electricity but is powered by laughter, the couple specialises in campfire singalongs, massages and inspiring a passion for horseriding. "I could while away the rest of my life on the Murray River, no problem," Padge said. "This place just speaks to me."

The life-giving irrigation conduit known as the Yarrawonga Main Channel (above) slices through farmland between Yarrawonga and Cobram, dispersing into a network of smaller channels, to deliver Murray water to the Murray Valley Irrigation Area of Victoria at a maximum rate of 3100 megalitres a day. Downstream, ordered plantings of parsnip seedlings (right) also drink from the Murray at the Kelly Brothers Market Gardens, which occupy 400 ha of river frontage.

Elizabeth Hume, the widowed sister-in-law of explorer Hamilton Hume, became the district's first white settler when she built Byramine Homestead (left), west of Yarrawonga, in 1842. Listed by the National Trust, it is one of Victoria's oldest homesteads. Historical distinction also belongs to 2400 ha North Tuppal station near Tocumwal, where champion shearer Brett Cavanough clips a merino (below) in the 72-stand Tuppal shearing shed. Built in 1897, it is reputedly one of the oldest and largest shearing sheds in Australia.

Log fires in two cosy rooms crackled and spat as I admired Byramine's period furnishings, rendered all the more charming by the scent and dull glow of several kerosene lamps. "At night it loses the cracks and cobwebs and the house really twinkles," Lynne said. "But I don't like being here at night by myself ... sometimes I fancy the spirit of Lizzie is still here."

Skies over Tocumwal

I watched the 80 m rope that linked our glider to the single-engined tow plane uncoil, quiver and then whip tight. We were airborne in a moment. Cocooned in the glider's front seat, with Sportavia Soaring Centre pilot Don Escott sitting behind me, I was surprised at how quickly the altimeter hit 1000, then 2000, then 3000 feet (914 m) before Don instructed me to release the rope. The instant I pulled the yellow lever to sever our umbilical cord, the glider became quiet and we were free to soar.

Banking south over the NSW township of Tocumwal, 45 km north-west of Mulwala, we surveyed square brown parcels of harvested rice paddocks, a system of irrigation channels

■ Like a good boomerang, Jack Byham (above) has travelled vast distances but always comes back to his Murray River home at Cobram, in central-northern Victoria. A boomerang carver and collector of international renown and three times Australian spear-throwing champion, 79-year-old Jack has made an estimated 750,000 boomerangs in his lifetime and in 1960 became the country's first commercial boomerang exporter. "I spent 50 years travelling out to Aboriginal communities across Australia and boomerang making was like a passport around the world for me," said the bloke known locally as Murray River Man.

■ Glorious sunset views greet Sportavia Gliding Centre instructor Don Escott, in the rear seat, and writer Amanda Burdon as they soar (right) over the Murray near Tocumwal. More than 500 international and countless Australian pilots converge on the southern NSW town each year to take to the skies, lured by the spacious aerodrome, reliable thermals, wide open spaces and stunning vistas.

and spurs, a golden wheat stockpile awaiting transport at the railhead and then the Murray River, unfurling like an indigo ribbon. Dense broccoli-like clusters of red gums clung to its convoluted channel, and the low afternoon sun bleached the bones of trees strewn like matchsticks along its shoals.

At 2000 feet (610 m), Don capitalised on a small thermal – a column of warm, rising air – and our silver bird rose in a graceful arc. "You don't like flying through a thermal without taking it up," came Don's deep voice through the headphones. "The sandbars on the Murray heat up in summer and you can often get good lift over the river. You never get just one thermal. If it's hot, you can climb them like you're going up in a lift. It's the only way to travel. And this is one of the best panoramas in the country."

Back on the ground later, still reeling from my aerial adventure, I learnt that the 500 or so international glider pilots from 26 countries who gather here each year are but the latest in a long line of aviators who have taken to Tocumwal's skies. The small town's aerodrome, built in 14 hasty weeks in 1942 to serve as a base for the US Army Air Corps, was the largest landing field in the Southern Hemisphere while in operation. It remains the largest World War II-vintage aerodrome still in use in Australia.

▓ Members of the 1st Base Ammunition Depot unload ammunition cases (above left) at the Tocumwal air base in May 1944 while two Women's Auxiliary Air Force armourers (above) clean the perspex gun turret of a B-24 Liberator bomber at the No. 7 Operational Training Unit. Tocumwal's 25 sq. km aerodrome, built in 1942 as a base for the US Army Air Corps, was the largest landing field in the Southern Hemisphere while in operation. More than 7000 American servicemen spent some of their time there during World War II before it became an RAAF training base and storage and repair depot, with a peak strength of 5000 personnel, before the RAAF finally left in October 1960.

Surrogate koala parents Peter and Margaret Webb, pictured with mischievous Missy and Strosity, have been caring for these cuddly orphans for several years at their home on Ulupna Island, near Strathmerton. "They'd be wonderful pets except that you can't house-train them," said Peter. "They snuggle up to you if you pick them up but they still have a mind of their own." Missy came into their care after a devastating plague of skeletoniser caterpillars stripped the area's red gums of most of their leaves four years ago, starving a large number of the island's koalas, including Missy's mother. The population is now recovering, and some individuals have dispersed east as far as Cobram and west to Echuca.

In the Sportavia Soaring Centre's bar, Tocumwal Historic Aerodrome Museum (THAM) spokesman Bob Brown explained that the aerodrome, formerly known as McIntyre Field, once covered 25 sq. km. It had 450 buildings, seven hangars, nearly 100 km of roadway, four runways, workshops and a 200-bed hospital hidden in a nearby forest. Over 7000 American servicemen spent time there during the war.

"Tocumwal was once part of the front-line defence of Australia," Bob said. "A line was drawn between Brisbane and Melbourne to mark the area that the Australian military was confident it could defend against the advancing Japanese. Along this front-line, called the Brisbane Line, they needed large airfields. Tocumwal was selected because of its flat, open terrain, distance from the coast and transport facilities."

But the aerodrome's defence role was short-lived. After the battle of the Coral Sea and successful campaigns in Papua New Guinea halted Japan's advance, the Americans moved north to Townsville. The Royal Australian Air Force (RAAF) took over the Tocumwal aerodrome soon afterwards for use as a Liberator bomber training base, storage and repair depot. Until October 1960 it housed 5000 RAAF personnel, including 400 Women's Auxiliary Australian Air Force (WAAF) members, and served as the final parking bay for hundreds of old warplanes, 700 of which were stripped and melted down for scrap or burnt.

But the contributions of these men, women and machines have not been forgotten. THAM has been piecing together their stories and is compiling an oral and photographic record with the aim of opening a museum that will give the organisation a more concrete form. "The aerodrome is a major part of Tocumwal even today, and we owe it to these people to preserve their history," said Bob.

Enduring forests

About 80 km downstream, in the enchanting Barmah forest, historical landmarks of a more ancient kind abound. I toured the forest's north-eastern corner with forester Mick Caldwell, a bearded bushranger of a bloke who has worked for 14 years supervising timber harvesting there. Mick described how, as a younger man, he used to ride through the forest on a horse – something he still does when marking trees for selective felling. Every now and then he's still stopped in his tracks by gum giants he's never seen before, some more than 500 years old. Twenty such trees are on the National Trust register.

"It's a pity they can't talk; they'd tell you some stories," said Mick, whose father was also a Barmah forester in the 1960s. "They've all got their own characters, not like in a pine plantation. I don't think we should cut down all the trees we're told we can. It's important to leave something for tomorrow. There are trees here that I'd like my grandchildren to see. I sometimes have a sense of them talking to you, they're so healthy, vibrant and vigorous."

Combined, the Barmah and Millewa forests cover some 70,000 verdant hectares and constitute the largest river red gum forest in Australia. It is one of the Murray River's enduring icons. Barmah forest was declared a reserve in 1908, when it was threatened by the

A grey day dawns on Barmah State Park as fishermen David Tanner and Keith Dobie prepare to launch *The Good Ship Venus* from the Barmah Lakes camping ground. David has been fishing here regularly for more than a decade and on this occasion was using worms called South African night crawlers as bait in his quest for a Murray cod. The 7900 ha park, containing 70 km of Murray River frontage, is a popular recreation area for fishers, waterskiers, paddlers and campers. Eastern grey kangaroos, emus and koalas, as well as some 220 bird species, have been recorded in the park and adjoining Barmah State Forest.

timber-hungry riverboats based at Echuca, 45 km to the south-west. Mick explained that logging – by four sawmills, six sleeper cutters, 12 commercial and scores of private firewood collectors – continues today but is carefully controlled to ensure the sustainability of the forest and protect the plants and animals that share the floodplain.

I was visiting in late autumn and we practically had the forest's dry paths to ourselves. The trees wore a muted green and brown livery and the river that sustains them had lost metres from its broad hips. But during a flood, when the river's water intrudes deep into the forest, the landscape dons a more vivacious dress.

"Flood time is absolutely brilliant," Mick said. "I have never been to Kakadu but I'd be game enough to say that this equals Kakadu. One day the forest is dry, the next it's a foot [30 cm] under water and the next it's three feet [1 m] under. The health of the plants and animals seems to improve overnight."

Barely 40 m wide in places and littered with fallen red gums, the aptly named Barmah Choke (above) is one of the narrower passages on the Murray. During a high river the bottleneck routinely overflows and spills water into a connecting network of lakes and wetlands in the Barmah forest, ensuring the continued growth of flood-dependent red gums.

RIVER SENTINELS

The tortured forms of river red gums are as synonymous with Australian rivers as the piercing screeches of corellas. River red gums (*Eucalyptus camaldulensis*) cover some 196,000 ha of the Murray floodplain, the most notable stands being in Barmah, Millewa, Moira, Gulpa Island, Perricoota, Koondrook, Campbells Island, Gunbower Island, Benwell Guttrum and Nyah–Vinifera forests.

The river red gum is Australia's only flood-tolerant eucalypt and its most widely distributed. Long before humans came to appreciate it for its accessible, durable, richly-coloured and termite-resistant timber, animals were seeking it out for shelter and food.

Bats, possums, gliders, snakes and birds, more than 100 species in all, use it in one way or another.

Known as one of the "great engines of floodplain ecology", the red gum provides vital energy and carbon to the river system through the dead foliage it drops and the timber it leaves behind when it dies. Its roots also help stabilise the river's banks.

It grows best when flooded every year, preferably in winter, for a few months and needs water to reproduce itself: a flood carries its seeds to high ground and saplings emerge before the next inundation.

In a well-watered forest, red gums can grow to 45 m with long straight trunks; in drier, more open woodland they tend to develop thick trunks, spreading crowns and large branches. They shed their leaves to reduce water loss during drought and in very hot weather they may drop branches without warning. So watch where you're walking and camping!

The Murray's mirror-like surface (left) reflects the health of a grand stand of red gums south of Corowa. Downstream, in the Barmah forest, many such trees fell victim to loggers before it was declared a reserve in 1908. Logs were chained to barges outrigger-style and escorted by bargemen (below) to the Echuca sawmills.

PADDLE-STEAMERS AND MALLEE
Echuca to the South Australian border

In a boatyard cluttered with machinery and materials at Echuca, the scene was paradoxically quiet. Heritage shipwrights Kevin Hutchison and Adam Auditori straddled a hefty slab of salmon-pink timber, their faces taut with concentration as they carefully drove their chisels along pencilled lines. With each painstaking incision, the groove in the red gum block sank deeper and the pile of curly shavings grew at their feet. Mesmerised by the "shark, shark, sharking" of the chiselled timber, I was transported to another time.

It's a journey that many visitors make at Echuca, where the beautifully restored wharf recalls life in the 19th century. It was a time when this was Australia's largest inland port, the centre of the red gum industry and a critical terminus for the rail from Melbourne. Horse-drawn vehicles trundle the dirt streets of the town's historic Port of Echuca; traditions are recalled in hissing steam displays; and costumed staff add an air of authenticity. But it is the grand paddle-steamers of yesteryear that possess the greatest mystique.

The port's operating fleet comprises four vessels (three steamers and a logging barge) that Kevin and his team have restored. The presence of the shipwrights themselves – both as "working exhibits" and as captains of the vessels they resurrected – adds to the visitors' experience.

I was lucky enough to meet Kevin and Adam while they were working on a restoration – that of the *Hero*, a 28 m steamer built at Echuca in 1874 and now back home, courtesy of a local businessman and steam buff. Not fond of idle conversation, Kevin explained that the timber they were gently fashioning was to become the *Hero*'s stem post, or breastplate. "It's the first part of the boat you see at the bow and all the hull boards are fastened to it," he said.

The vessel, which caught fire and sank at Boundary Bend in 1957, waited on a cradle nearby to become Kevin's sixth restoration in 25 years. It had been stripped back to its bare bones, a collection of steel ribs bound by just a few weathered timbers.

Working only from old photographs, Kevin and Adam would rebuild the steamer plank by plank, using age-old techniques and tools, immeasurable skill and an inordinate dose of patience. "If you work with old materials and old techniques, you have less chance of failure," said Kevin, who is as unassuming as the dormant river workhorses he reawakens, only a handful of which survived beyond the early 1900s.

Exuding steam and romance, the PS *Adelaide* (opposite) majestically rounds Hairpin Bend below Echuca, its home port. The oldest wooden-hulled paddle-steamer still operating in the world, the *Adelaide* was built in 1866 and worked until 1957, mainly towing logging barges between Barmah forest and Echuca. It sat in an Echuca park for many years before undergoing a four-year restoration and making a triumphant return to the Murray in 1985. These days it ventures out only once or twice a month.

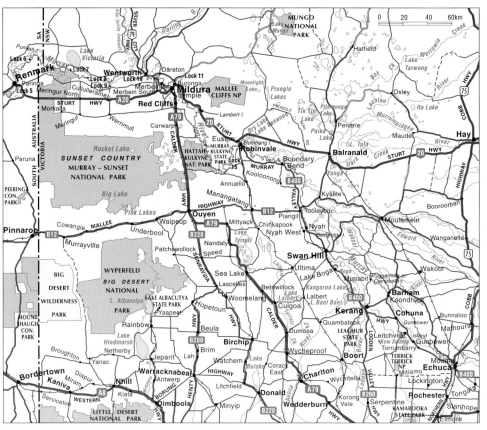

"The boats experienced a bit of a resurgence during the 1956 floods, when they were again used to cart firewood and wool to Echuca and the *Hero* rescued cattle stranded by floodwaters, but as soon as the river went down the paddleboat trade let out its last gasp," he said. "It's satisfying to see them finally go down the river again after all your hard work."

On the deck of the restored *Alexander Arbuthnot* earlier in the day, I'd closed my eyes to tune in to the symphony of sounds the boat made as we steamed upstream of Echuca. First the crackle of the burning timber as flames filled the firebox, then the hiss of steam escaping from the bubbling boiler, the repetitive throbbing of the engine and finally the thrashing of the side-wheels as they sliced through the sage-green water.

With bearded captain Neil Hutchison (Kevin's son), dressed in a trilby hat, woollen waist-coat and work pants, at the helm, it was easy to imagine that the "*AA*" was on its way to the Barmah forest to collect a load of logs. The last traditional cargo steamer built on the

Murray – in 1923, for Arbuthnot Sawmills at Koondrook – it routinely towed timber-laden barges. After its last job, carting a load of charcoal and firewood from Barmah for Melbourne's gas production and factory boilers, it ceased operating in 1943 and sank in 1947.

"What these boats have been through in their lifetimes is extraordinary," Neil said when I visited him in the wheelhouse. "Of the 260 boats once based here at Echuca, only three are left (including the *Hero*) that haven't been butchered. The AA's one of the port's lesser lights and a bit slow, but she's easy to work; you treat her like a lady and she'll treat you right. She's quiet, not like a thumping modern engine that vibrates and rattles. I like to hear the chuffing of the engine echoing off the banks."

Returning to port after our one-hour cruise, I noticed three tiny watercraft tied up to the riverbank by the wharf. It wasn't until late that afternoon, after leaving Kevin to continue his work in the shipyard, that Bill and I managed to track down the owners of the three Canadian canoes, the Byrne family of far-north Queensland.

Dawn and Mal Byrne had long been fascinated by the Murray and wanted to explore it with their four children, Brooke, 15, Kyle, 12, Jesse, 7, and Jack, 6. With sponsorship from AUSTRALIAN GEOGRAPHIC, they gave up their comfortable life at Airlie Beach, bought the canoes, and headed for Corowa. There they sold their car and, having never paddled before, set off down the river the next day. They'd covered 364 km and would take "as long as it takes" to reach the Coorong in SA during what promised to be the journey of a lifetime.

▦ Heritage shipwright Kevin Hutchinson (opposite) inspects the newly installed stem post of the 28 m steamer *Hero*, his sixth restoration in 25 years at the Port of Echuca, which revels in reliving the glory days of the river trade. Every bit the river captain, Kevin's son Neil (above left) guides the *Alexander Arbuthnot* on one of its regular passenger outings, while engineer Tony Brown (above) stokes the boiler, which burns a tonne of timber a day.

Originally 332 m long, Echuca's red-gum wharf had three levels to allow for the variation between winter and summer river heights, sometimes as much as 8.5 m. An ageing flood marker (above) graphically shows that despite its height the wharf was still susceptible to flooding, largely because the Goulburn and Campaspe rivers enter the Murray on either side of the town. Most of the Murray's paddle-steamers had shallow draughts so they could keep going even when the river level fell to barely 2 m. Those that plied the reaches above Mildura bore the Top End flag (opposite); Bottom-enders, the steamers that went down to Goolwa, flew a different standard. Competition between the two camps for contracts was fierce and skippers were forever racing – to beat falling or to catch rising rivers and to deliver passengers and cargo on time.

Time was of little consequence to the Byrne family (right) of north Queensland, pictured near the Echuca wharf, when they set off to paddle the Murray from Corowa to the Southern Ocean in SA. "We're taking as long as it takes," said patriarch Mal Byrne. "I want the kids to experience a part of Australia that has largely been forgotten."

"It's the longest river in Australia and without it a lot of the inland would never have been opened up," Mal said. "I want the kids to experience a part of Australia that has largely been forgotten. The whole point is not to rush, but to cruise past and enjoy everything. We eat when we're hungry and sleep when we're tired."

It was clear from my brief riverbank conversation with young Jesse, a keen twitcher who could proudly name all the bird species he'd encountered, that the Murray was a talented teacher.

"We've paddled right up to a flock of black swans, seen koalas in the wild, slept in donkey paddocks and learnt a lot about the night sky," Dawn said. "I think the kids are realising that the river is something we all must take care of."

Island of red gums

I'd been humbled by many a red gum on my river travels, but none compared with the one that dwarfed me on Gunbower Island, introduced to me by 79-year-old Peter Disher.

Born and bred in Barham, NSW, Koondrook's sister town across the river, Peter has had a passion for birds since the age of six. It follows that he should also take more than a passing interest in trees.

I'd heard tales about the noble Gunbower individual, but its exact location was a fiercely guarded secret. There was little threat of me disclosing its whereabouts; I was lost the moment Peter turned off the main road into the island's maze of dirt tracks.

Echuca chef Paul Jarman (above), co-owner of Oscar W's Restaurant, serves up a local delicacy – steamed yabbies prepared with a saffron mayonnaise and shaved fennel. Most of the yabbies on his menu come from Aquafarms Australia at nearby Moama. Covering 52 ha, Aquafarms is Australia's largest commercial yabby producer. Their well-drilled dog Taras (right) helps assistant manager Scott Peck and gumbooted manager Paul Lavars retrieve nets beyond their reach.

At approximately 50 km long, Gunbower is the largest inland island in Australia. It is a low-lying floodplain bordered on its north by the Murray River and on its south by Gunbower Creek. It is cloaked in red gum and box 80 per cent of it is inside 19,440 ha Gunbower State Forest. Although a handful of timber-getters continue to work on the island, as they have for 120 years, it is better known today as an environmental and recreational haven. Its tranquil wetlands, fringed by reeds and rushes, are recognised under the Ramsar Convention as being of international importance. They are home to rare species such as the broad-shelled turtle and echo to the calls of the barking marsh frog in spring. The anglers, canoeists and walkers who enjoy the island's quiet backwaters might also be lucky enough to spot a white-bellied sea-eagle plunging from the sky to snatch a fish from one of its waterways.

There was no such spectacle on the day of our visit, but the Eagle's Nest Tree was more than ample compensation. "She's a beauty all right," was Peter's assessment. While it lacks the thick crown and wide-spreading limbs of more symmetrical specimens, this giant red gum stands 50.6 m high and, 1 m from the ground, is almost 10 m around the trunk. Craning my neck, I saw that it bore a tangle of sticks in its canopy (hence its name), but while white-plumed honeyeaters and brown treecreepers flitted around its base, there was no sign of the wedge-tailed eagle that built this eyrie.

Only Arbuthnot Sawmills, established in 1889, is still licensed to harvest timber in Gunbower State Forest. The mill's staff respect their long-held privilege. Huge bench saws whirred and barked as I looked over the mill with manager Paul Madden. In its heyday, the mill employed 200 people in timber-getting, sawmilling and shipbuilding. At the abandoned slip at the rear of the timber yard, Paul pointed to where 12 steamers and barges were built, including the town's namesake, which could carry 200 tonnes of cargo.

"Today we employ 20 people and we mill just as much timber," Paul said. "The timber industry is extremely important to these small communities, and we're still the largest employer in Koondrook. These red gum forests have been logged sustainably for over 150 years."

While the mill produces traditional tongue-and-groove flooring and wood panelling, and supplies sawn timber for housing and landscaping, it is increasing the volume of kiln-dried red gum for high-class furniture. As Bill and I explored Koondrook, we saw examples of this furniture in a series of showrooms: solid cabinets, tables and dining chairs, all highly polished to enhance their rich red hue.

History revived

Black swans are rare in Swan Hill today, but they were clearly abundant in 1836 when Major Thomas Mitchell camped on a sandy rise near the river during his 2100 km journey from Sydney to Portland. Swans nesting on a nearby lagoon disturbed his sleep with their trumpeting and gave the town its name. But the prospect of sleepless nights did not deter the settlers who promptly followed in Mitchell's footsteps. Within 10 years more than six large sheep stations had been established in the district.

A lagoon on Perricoota station, about 70 km downstream of Moama, provides a haven for 75 houseboats at Deep Creek Marina. It's about six hours by boat from here to Echuca, but few of the Melbourne-based houseboat-owners stray that far. "They normally head for the first sandbank they come across," said marina manager Anthony Watson. "When there's enough water below Torrumbarry Weir [32 km downstream], some travel into SA."

At its peak, Arbuthnot Sawmills of Koondrook, in central-northern Victoria, employed 200 people in timber-getting, sawmilling and shipbuilding. Today bench-saw operator Norbert Terpkovitz (above), shown milling red-gum flitches into usable sizes, is one of 20 staff maintaining a tradition begun in 1889. Like Murray River Sawmills, upstream at Echuca, Arbuthnots is increasing its production of kiln-dried red gum for furniture manufacturing. "It's the future of the business and it's growing," said Murray River Sawmills manager Owen Chalmers (right), pictured marking red-gum logs in the mill yard, which feeds about 8000 tonnes of timber to the mill a year. "Red gum is becoming more of a prized item."

An afternoon in the open-air museum known as the Swan Hill Pioneer Settlement, set on the promontory of land within Horseshoe Bend, offered me insights into the struggles those pioneers faced as they tamed the rugged inland. Clearing the deep-rooted mallee was back-breaking work, but muscle was matched by resourcefulness and small communities quickly grew from humble beginnings.

Wandering along the dirt roads of the 3 ha settlement, where Clydesdale-drawn carriages and vintage cars are as common as pedestrians, I called in at the Cobb & Co. stables, the 1860 post office and the archetypal bush school before heading for the blacksmith's shop and saddlery, where time-honoured techniques are still used. Fat white hens scratched about in the garden at Towaninnie Homestead, a drop-log construction dating from 1888, and the rollicking riverboat days were remembered in the sparsely furnished reproduction of the Lower Murray Inn. Given the size of the portable prison cell, I reckoned few revellers would have fancied a night in the lockup.

In celebrating the initiative of the "mallee mob", the pioneer settlement gives due credit to the part agricultural implements and machinery played. It contains an early example of the stump-jump plough, which revolutionised mallee-country farming; possibly Australia's first combine harvester; and one of the best collections of steel-wheel tractors in the country, 23 specimens in all. Wearing mutton-chop whiskers befitting the era, technician Newton Williams was only too happy to show me what is thought to be Australia's most historically significant tractor, a rare three-wheel-drive 1907 Sanderson.

Ruby hues fill the showroom of River Redgum Furniture (left), one of several Koondrook businesses specialising in handicrafts and furnishings made from the sturdy local timber. Sophisticated drying techniques, taking as long as six months, coupled with air drying, make red gum stable enough for high-class furniture. Craftsman Colin Bray of Natural Edge, taking a call (below) in the red-gum phone booth he and Dean Atwell, at left, fashioned from a blackened stump for a Melbourne hotel, has no hang-ups about a more rustic look.

I concluded my visit by looking over the paddle-steamer *Pyap*, which makes regular cruises from the Horseshoe Bend Wharf. Built in 1896 as a barge and converted to a floating shop in 1906, the *Pyap* sold everything imaginable to customers at 60 landings between Murray Bridge and Morgan, in SA, for 20 years.

Just across the way rested another Murray madam: the largest paddle-steamer to ply the river in its day, the passenger vessel *Gem*, which is undergoing restoration. Dubbed the "Queen of the Murray", it operated tirelessly from 1876 to 1952.

One man who knows the *Gem* more intimately than most is Bill Hogg, the son of one of the last of the paddleboat men, Paddy Hogg. Bill lived aboard the *Gem* as a child, and when the vessel was bought by the Swan Hill community in 1962 and had to be towed back from Mildura, his father won the contract. Bill celebrated his 21st birthday on board.

"I'm one of the luckiest blokes around," he'd told me the previous day on the deck of his tour boat, the *Kookaburra*, docked just downstream of Swan Hill. "From six years old, except for 10 years, I've spent my life on the river and I got the tail end of the old river men. The river was the love of Paddy's life; it always came first. He was 85 when he died and there's a Murray River flag flying on his grave."

Time slows to the clopping pace of Clydesdales at the Swan Hill Pioneer Settlement in central-northern Victoria (above), where horse-drawn vehicle rides are a popular attraction. "The settlement preserves and maintains history and it also made history by becoming the first outdoor museum in Australia when it opened in 1966." The 3 ha complex has more than 50 buildings and exhibits, including one of the best collections of steel-wheel tractors in Australia, faithfully maintained by Newton Williams (opposite). "It's the jewel in our crown," said Newton of this rare three-wheel-drive Sanderson Model A tractor, built in 1907 and imported the following year.

A MAN CALLED POSSUM

The Murray River has been home to some colourful travellers in its time, but few can have been humbler and more self-sufficient than David James Jones, the man they simply called "Possum".

A former New Zealand shearer who settled in Australia in the 1920s, Possum fell on hard times and went bush in 1928. Unable to find station work and denied a ration ticket during the Depression, he spurned society and lived as a recluse for the next 54 years on the river between Wentworth and Renmark.

Possum eschewed all modern conveniences. He established a number of camp sites along the river – in hollow logs, under trees, on saltbush flats and beside billabongs – and lived on fish, yabbies, mussels, rabbits, feral cats, foxes, birds and their eggs, and native spinach.

He was extremely shy and rarely spoke but would regularly appear at remote stations and cut firewood, expecting little more in return than salt, matches and the occasional newspaper.

It was Possum's capacity for hard work and his way with animals that so impressed the few who knew him. He would tend sick or injured animals and routinely crutch flyblown sheep or rescue them from muddy watercourses. He would toil for days, unasked, removing burrs or cutting bush for drought-affected stock, drenching sheep, mending fences and gates or tidying outstations.

We know of Possum's exploits thanks to the curiosity and compassion of retired police detective sergeant Max Jones, of Renmark, who developed an unlikely friendship with him over 30 years and immortalised his reminiscences in a book titled *A Man Called Possum*.

"The people who met Possum didn't understand him, but they knew he was gentle and kind and they respected his independence," Max said. "Sometimes he'd travel the rivers for months. He explored as far as Bourke on the Darling, Wagga on the Murrumbidgee and to Albury on the Murray, and walked from Lake Victoria to the Murray mouth twice. Most people were surprised at how he survived all those years. He must have known the Murray's every bend and curve."

Possum died in 1982, aged 81. His headstone in a small private graveyard nearby reads: "At rest where he roamed".

A likable chap with a devilish grin and lively eyes, Bill introduces the Murray to new generations of river-farers during his daily cruises. When Bill and I hopped aboard, a good crowd was waiting to enjoy his informative commentary, peppered with references to the long-gone riverboat captains, even the most respectable of whom seemed to possess an outlaw streak. Of them Ernestine Hill wrote in her book *Water Into Gold*: "They read the river as an open book, learned it and loved it, and spent their lives on it, faithful to the trust through flood and fall." Author E.M. (Mick) Kelsall was more frank in *A Riverman's Story*: "People look at the restored *Adelaide* or the *B22* and see a paddleboat or an outrigger barge. I see ghosts, colourful, hard-living, hard-swearing ghosts."

Bill proudly admits that his father fell into the latter category. Yet Bill had no hesitation in following in his wake. "I couldn't imagine doing anything else. I'm the last generation of those traditional riverboat captains and I've got a tradition to uphold. It doesn't matter where I go on the Murray; I know Paddy's been there, and that's a good feeling."

Though barely 19 km separates them by road, Murray Downs Homestead (above) and the older Tyntyndyer Homestead (above right) are worlds apart in size and architectural style. Established in 1866 just 3 km north-east of Swan Hill, Murray Downs was a grand estate occupying 32,400 ha, complete with a 20-room mansion, extensive formal gardens, its own school, store and church. Tyntyndyer Homestead, in contrast, features drop-log walls and simpler furnishings befitting the more pragmatic Beveridge family that took up 78,000 ha in 1846, in the days when building materials could be transported only by bullock dray.

Angler Jamie Petrowsky, of Kerang, tries his luck (opposite) as the Speewa Ferry makes a routine trip across the Murray near Piangil, in north-western Victoria. The ferry, one of only two that still work the river in NSW/Victoria, makes about 80 crossings a day.

Rewards of the river

In the delightful children's classic *Wind in the Willows*, Ratty is awfully fond of river adventures. "There is *nothing* – absolutely nothing – half so much worth doing as simply messing about in boats," he says. This passage came back to me as I watched two riverboats glide round a bend in the Murray 45 km downstream of Swan Hill and pull ashore near us.

Bill and I encountered the caravan-sized vessel and its smaller but plumper timber cohort near the township of Piangil as we continued on our own river adventure. Fancying we'd found some genuine river rats, we scrambled down the bank to meet them.

We were greeted by Russell Anderson, skipper of the *Gypsy Ellen*, the larger vessel. With his wild hair and long grey beard, Russell lived up to our expectations. He had teamed up with the crew of the side-wheeler *Tina* – Dave Morgan, his partner Lisa O'Keefe and their blond daughter Alysia, 4 – for three months of Murray meandering. Both vessels were low on diesel and Alysia was itching to stretch her legs on the riverbank with her cattle dog, Molly, so they'd stopped for a spell.

Smarting from a marriage breakdown and a back injury, Russell had sold his farm at Torrumbarry, downstream of Echuca, and bought the boat a year ago. He hasn't looked back. "I just like sitting here watching the water go by," he said as he slowly rolled a ciga-rette. "There are no bills, no lawn-mowing, and the council collects your rubbish. It's just

me and my solitude. It's the freedom of river life that appeals to me, and we're lucky to have it in Australia."

Dave Morgan, by contrast, has made the river his life for the best part of a decade. As thin as a bootlace, he has the far-off gaze, beard and steely reserve of a sea-captain and was reluctantly heading back to his home port of Swan Hill after a four-month journey. It was his and Lisa's last hurrah before settling Alysia into school, and they were enjoying every moment.

"I've learnt to read the river pretty well," Dave said when I asked about the daily hazards. "It's in my blood now; I don't intend to ever leave the river. I don't think I'll ever have a house; I would rather have ropes. We go anywhere that the boat will go."

While Bill drove Lisa, Alysia and Russell into town to buy fuel, Dave and I chatted over a cup of tea in *Tina's* wheelhouse. Alysia's toys littered the floor and washing hung from a clothesline strung across the rear deck, where Lisa's fishing rods poked expectantly out over the river. Their lives moved to the Murray's rhythm and I found myself envying them their independence. Alluding to business and personal problems, Dave confided that he "would have gone mental if not for the river", and he showed me a balsa model of the boat he dreams of building. "If I can find a way of making a living on the river I will," he said resolutely.

▩ Muted tones and strong textures provide inspiration for artist Margaret Lewis (above), seen here with her dog, Cassie, as she sketches near her home at Piangil, in north-western Victoria. "I'm often commissioned to produce paintings featuring the river and it's a common subject for my art students," she said. "Red gum-lined rivers are synonymous with Australia and this is a very ancient one." The Murray's age-old character is similarly alluring to a swag of adventurous river gypsies such as the travellers aboard the *Tina* and the *Gypsy Ellen* (right) – Alysia Morgan, her parents Lisa O'Keefe and Dave Morgan and fellow river rat Russell Anderson – pictured near Piangil during a refuelling stop. Despite such perfunctory tasks and having to be constantly alert for snags and other obstacles, river ramblers value the peace and freedom the lifestyle affords. "Anybody who has lived on the Murray for a time comes to love it," said Dave.

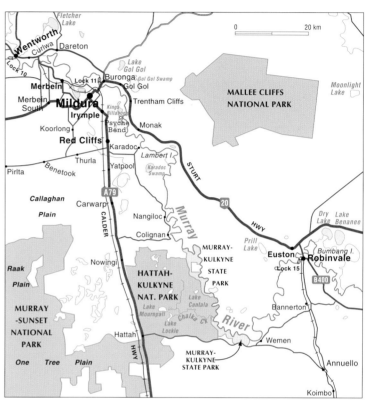

Irrigation from the Murray has transformed cleared mallee country in the Sunraysia district of north-western Victoria into a lush 35,000 ha fabric (left) embroidered with vineyards, market gardens and orchards worth $1 billion annually to the Victorian economy. It's a far cry from the drought-ravaged Mildura sheep run, described in a newspaper of the day as a "Sahara of hissing hot winds, and red driving sand... a carrion-polluted wilderness", that greeted the pioneering Chaffey brothers in 1886.

Making an ecologically sustainable living today are organic and biodynamic winemaker Steven Caracatsanoudis and his mother Stavroula (above), of Robinvale Wines. Sound irrigation practices are just as important to the Riverfarm Vegetables operation, where pickers cut broccoli (right).

If he's successful, Dave will follow countless others drawn from all over the world by the lifestyle and prosperity the Murray River promises. This cultural diversity is strikingly evident in the families who tend manicured fields along the Murray around Robinvale, to the north-west, and further downstream at the modern city of Mildura.

Just south of Robinvale, Bill and I called in at the region's only organic winery to meet a family familiar with hard work. At Robinvale Wines, an impressive white building modelled on a Greek temple soars up out of a sea of grapevines. This is the heart of the Caracatsanoudis family's business – organically and biodynamically grown grapes.

Matriarch Stavroula Caracatsanoudis barely clears the top of the cellar-door counter where she greets customers with a smile alive with old-world generosity. She was just 22 and pregnant with her eldest son, Steve, when she emigrated from Greece to Australia with her late husband, George, in 1954. They moved to Robinvale in 1969 "for the quiet life and the warm weather" and to fulfil George's dream of establishing a vineyard. It's a dream that Stavroula, Steve and her second son, Bill, are now realising.

"My father started pulling out orange trees and planting vines in 1975 and now we have 75 acres [30 ha] under vines – half table grapes and half wine grapes – irrigated from the Murray River," said Steve, the manager of Robinvale Wines, as Stavroula plied Bill and me with delicious grape juice. "We make dried fruit, pure juice, alcoholic and

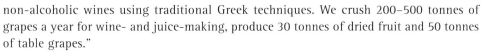

non-alcoholic wines using traditional Greek techniques. We crush 200–500 tonnes of grapes a year for wine- and juice-making, produce 30 tonnes of dried fruit and 50 tonnes of table grapes."

Strolling through a vineyard with Steve later, I noticed the rich green growth between the spidery vines. He explained that instead of spraying weeds with chemicals and leaving these corridors barren, as happens elsewhere, his family plants clover and vetch that fix nitrogen from the air and naturally replenish the soil's nutrient levels. Avoiding chemical spraying also protects the natural insect predators.

"Traditionally, everyone farmed this way," said Steve, whose face is etched with its own furrows. "We really are the normal farmers and everyone else is unconventional in the chemicals they use." Without the aid of artificial fertilisers, the Caracatsanoudises rely on compost to feed the soil, creating humus that feeds the plants naturally. They are especially vigilant about what drains from their property back into the river.

"Organic methods are very labour-intensive and more expensive but we strive to have the least impact on the river we can," Steve said. "It's a hard row to hoe but we do it for health, environmental and sustainability reasons. It's not just for my children; it's for the community, the consumer, the planet. Towns have prospered because of the river. Now they are going to have to do something for it or change their ways to protect its health."

Observing a time-honoured Italian tradition, Mildura horticulturists Gino and Elina Garreffa dedicate three days each June to making the family's annual supply of salami, prosciutto and capicola, which they cure in an airy shed (above left). The couple migrated with their parents from southern Italy in the 1950s and '60s, met in Mildura, married, and now run a diverse 21 ha table-grape, olive-oil and fruit farm. Most of their olives find their way into the cold presses of Gianni Grigoletto (above), a former industrial chemist from a family of Italian winemakers who bottles the oil for a number of local growers. "We have a hot, dry climate here and lots of water, like in Calabria, and the olives grow well," Gianni said. "But only about 200 tonnes of olives are harvested in Sunraysia each year, so it's still a small industry."

The day is done and citrus worker Jack Alexander wets a line and his throat in Hattah-Kulkyne NP, near Colignan, in north-western Victoria. Just 75 km by road south of Mildura, the 48,000 ha park caters to 80,000 visitors a year, many of whom enjoy swimming, windsurfing and canoeing in its 17 ephemeral lakes, fed by the Murray.

Hattah-Kulkyne National Park

It was a chill winter morning. Veils of chiffon mist shrouded the red gums along the dry bed of Chalka Creek, about 90 km downstream of Robinvale. I stood in silence on a burnt-orange sand dune with Hattah-Kulkyne National Park ranger Andy Wise and watched the veils waver ever so slightly in the breeze and settle in the creek's depression. Kangaroo tracks in the dew-damp sand showed we were not the only ones up and about this early.

"Chalka Creek is the vital link; if it wasn't for this anabranch of the Murray there would be no lakes," Andy said, breaking my reverie. "When the Murray River is in flood, the Chalka funnels the water into the lake system, and when the river recedes, the water drains out of both ends. The cycle of drying and refilling keeps these temporary wetlands productive."

During its long passage, the Murray courses through landscapes of vastly different topography, altitude, climate and soil type. Nowhere is the soil and vegetation variety more striking than in 48,000 ha Hattah-Kulkyne National Park, a popular place for walkers, birdwatchers and canoeists. The park holds a broad sampling of Murray habitat including floodplain, sand dunes, box woodlands, 17 freshwater lakes, often dry for several seasons, and mallee.

Andy said regent parrots, listed as vulnerable, are locally plentiful there and malleefowl are around but elusive. I can personally attest to the park's wealth of red-rumped parrots, corellas, timid rosellas, mallee ringnecks and white-winged choughs.

"The park is renowned worldwide for birdwatching," Andy said. "We get a lot of international visitors seeking out the mallee emu wren, which lives in a restricted area of spinifex in the north-west corner of Victoria and extending into South Australia."

▥ Ghostly fingers of mist reach through the red gums lining Chalka Creek (top), the Murray River anabranch that feeds the lakes of Hattah-Kulkyne NP. An important habitat for waterbirds in particular, the park supports more than 200 bird species overall including emus. This male (above) carefully tends his clutch of glossy eggs.

CARP — RABBIT OF THE RIVER

Australia's most abundant freshwater fish is also one of its most despised. It is the introduced carp, which has made itself at home in the Murray River and its tributaries.

Identified by the two barbels at each corner of its mouth, the carp was originally an Asian native but is now resident on all continents except Antarctica. Despite this, it is often known as the European carp. First released in Australia in the mid- to late 1800s, it didn't spread through the Murray–Darling Basin until the 1960s and '70s, when it was helped by further releases and floods. Today it is found throughout the basin and is well adapted to river regulation.

The carp has been blamed for everything from the disappearance of native fish and aquatic plants to the collapse of riverbanks and the muddying of river water, but whether it is a symptom or a cause of river degradation remains debatable.

What is indisputable is its tenacity. The carp is an efficient invader; it can tolerate poor water quality, low oxygen levels, high temperatures and salinity, and it breeds prolifically – a female can produce up to 300,000 eggs per kilogram of body weight.

The carp feeds voraciously on the river bed, sucking small invertebrates, detritus, shrimps and fish eggs from the mud. In high numbers it does increase the turbidity of water and uproots aquatic plants. On the positive side, young carp can make good food for larger native fish.

Current carp-control methods include a combination of improving river management to favour native species, harvesting carp for human consumption, and experimenting with chemicals and biological controls to inhibit their breeding. Carp are already used in liquid fertiliser, dry compost and pet food, and for yabby and rock-lobster bait.

When the lakes fill, twitchers can barely keep count of the ducks, magpie geese, pied stilts, red-necked avocets, egrets, spoonbills, ibis, cormorants and dotterels that touch down in their hundreds.

It wasn't just the birds that I found amazing. During a short walk through the mallee with Andy, I was equally surprised by the diversity of plant life; skeleton fan-flowers, desert grevillea, small orchids, flax lilies and the ubiquitous spinifex struggled up through the sandy soil. "Just about everything in the mallee grows slowly because of the tough conditions they have to tolerate," explained Andy. "The soils are low in nutrients, the climate is usually dry and the summers hot."

But it's precisely this combination of conditions that has ensured the success of many of the industries in nearby Sunraysia, the rich agricultural belt that straddles the Murray between Mildura and the SA border.

The spirits of the many Aboriginal people who once lived by its banks are evoked on this moody morning beside the Lindsay River (left), in the Murray-Sunset NP. In creating 1500 ha Lindsay Island to the Murray's south, the encircling Lindsay River ensured their peaceful isolation for thousands of years and now protects almost 500 of their burial sites. A monument to early European life in Mildura is *Rio Vista* (below), the original home of irrigation pioneer and city co-founder Ben Chaffey and now part of a regional museum.

Irrigating the mallee

Several days after leaving Hattah-Kulkyne I inspected the Psyche Bend Pumping Station, beautifully restored by the Sunraysia Steam Preservation Society. The pumping station was the hub of the fledgling irrigation industry that transformed a dust bowl into an inland oasis.

Commissioned in 1891, when Mildura was little more than a run-down mallee sheep station, Psyche Bend was one of the first pumping stations installed by the enterprising Canada-born brothers George and William (Ben) Chaffey. Its gleaming green triple-expansion steam engine, in its original brick housing, once drove three centrifugal pumps that each raised 159,100 litres of water a minute from the Murray in four "lifts" via Kings Billabong. "It was pumping water for only six months of the year, but the engine worked day and night," said society president Ian Kellett. The sturdy steam engine was still going strong more than 60 years later.

JOURNEY'S END
South Australian border to the sea

"Every great river gradually grows its own history, its own temperament, its own quite distinguishable personality." Author Lawrence Durrell wrote these words about the River Rhone, which swaggers 800 km from the Swiss Alps through south-eastern France to the Mediterranean. At three times the length of the Rhone, the great Murray River could be said to possess several distinct personalities. The wild youngster that leaves the Australian Alps undergoes a great deal of maturing during its westward progress through NSW and Victoria. By the time it reaches the SA border, it is self-assured and done with rushing.

At least this is how Bill and I found the river one summer morning on a pretty arc known as Plush's Bend, just outside Renmark in eastern SA near the SA–Victoria border. Light danced on the turgid brown water that traced a languid course through the tinder-dry Riverland. Waiting for us in his riverboat beside the boat ramp was Rod Coombs, third-generation Murray River commercial fisherman and director of the Riverland Fishermans' Association (RFA). Wearing bright blue overalls and equally gaudy red gloves, his freckled face shaded by a cap, Rod, 53, had been on the river since 5 a.m. and his freezer tub was already full of callop and carp destined for Sydney and Melbourne markets. After welcoming us aboard, he motored downstream to retrieve the last of his drum- and yabby nets.

One of 30 licence-holders who fish between the SA border and Wellington, on the shores of Lake Alexandrina, Rod has been at the forefront of industry reform in recent years. He has helped implement new minimum catch sizes and restrictions on the quantity and type of gear fisherfolk can use in SA, and he has been actively campaigning for fish habitat protection. Salty water and carp are widely blamed for the degradation of the SA fishery, but Rod told me that he believes insensitive water management and excessive use of scarce water are the true villains.

"Fish tune in to the seasons; they read the cues," he said as we puttered along. "They sense that the water is on its way and they gear up to spawn or migrate, but if the water supply is cut off or diminished, it plays havoc with their biological clock. The people who regulate the river control the health of fish stocks – and our catches."

Beside a snag marked by a small buoy, Rod stopped the boat to check a large drum-net. Somewhere high above, a whistling kite uttered its rapid-fire call. The boat lurched to one side as Rod lifted the weighty catch. Flapping in the net were seven glistening callop of roughly the

Breakers greet the Murray River (opposite) as it meets the Southern Ocean on the south-eastern coast of SA. Having drained into Lake Alexandrina, visible in the background, the Murray is directed by a series of barrages around Hindmarsh Island before it can lose itself in the sea, concluding the languid journey that began in the Australian Alps.

The European carp may be a pest to many, but to third-generation commercial fisherman Rod Coombs it's a worthy catch. He finds premium table markets in Sydney and Melbourne for carp he catches near Renmark. "I'm not suggesting we need carp in the river but it's time people realised they're a very good eating fish, but need a little extra preparation," he said.

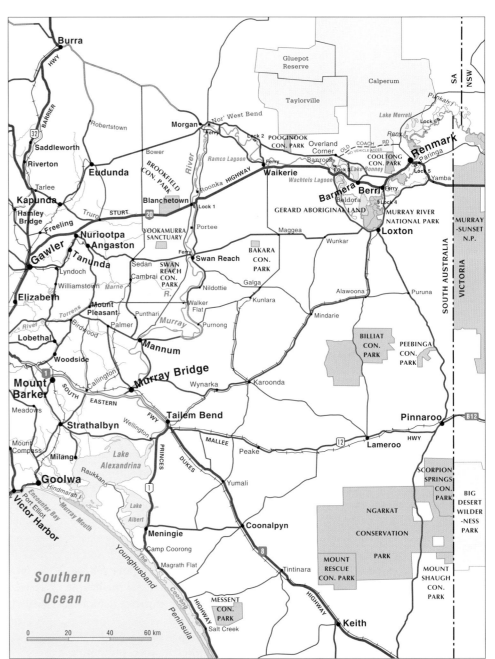

same size and a single carp, its large yellow scales resplendent in the sunshine. We emptied more carp from two other nets and a clutch of blue-black Murray crayfish from the yabby snare. There wasn't a single Murray cod in the morning's catch, but Rod said they are very street-smart fish. He's content just knowing they're still in the system.

"I get a lot of pleasure returning the big Murray cod to the river," he said. "The big old mothers can produce 100,000–500,000 eggs a year if conditions are right. You get to know them a bit like family. They're an indication that the system is still healthy."

In the Riverland district, a triangle extending west from Renmark as far as Morgan and 120 km southwards, it's not just the fish that depend on the Murray's condition. The health of $530 million worth of horticultural enterprises is also tuned to the river's rhythm. Emerging from the mallee, the river contracts in its valley to foster a prolific 30,000 ha nursery of grapevines, citrus and fruit and nut orchards. From the air, their well-ordered rows resemble the raised pile of green corduroy fabric. The Riverland produces half of SA's wine grapes (one-third of Australia's total), and one-third of the nation's citrus, with an estimated 2 million cartons exported to the USA in the year 2000.

The region is the home of Angas Park, Australia's largest processor of dried tree-fruits. At its processing plant in Loxton, 55 km south of Renmark, I watched hair-netted women removing stones from halved peaches nestled in timber trays. After this the trays would spend

Biologist Bryan Pierce and project officer Keith Hand (above left), from the South Australian Research and Development Institute, check a seine net for endangered native fish being protected, and re-established, in effluent ponds at the Murray Bridge Army base. They have worked closely with professional fisherman Garry Hera-Singh (above) to develop the commercial fishery in the Murray's lower Coorong lagoon.

■ Many hands make light work of de-stoning peaches (above) at the Angas Park fruit processing plant at Loxton, in SA's Riverland. After this the peaches spend a night in sulphur houses before being spread out in the sun to dry. "The girls who patrol the lawns retrieving any remaining stones are called the chooks," said maintenance supervisor Jack Battams (right).

the night in sulphur houses, where peaches are gassed with a sulphur-based chemical to preserve and enrich their natural colours. From there they would be moved to the nearby north-facing "green".

Stepping outside into the scorching sun, I marvelled at the magnificent orange lawn – tray after tray of peaches arranged under a scattered flock of sheepish clouds. There the peaches would sunbake for 2–3 days until they were dry enough to complete the shrivelling process under shade. Angas Park, which turns out some 4000 tonnes of dried tree-fruits a year, is the only company still using this natural drying method on such a large scale.

"We've had a good run this season," maintenance manager Jack Battams told me. "The fruit has been good, we've not had any rain and we've had a couple of weeks of temperatures over 40°C. We rely on the sun to grow the fruit and the sun to dry it, but without the Murray there wouldn't be anything.

Navigating the Riverland

Windsurfers skipped across the choppy surface of Lake Bonney in a breeze that had risen right on cue for the weekend sailing regatta. The foreshores of the splendid lake, which hangs off the Murray at Barmera, were cluttered with boats, trailers and bathers of every colour and dimension. It was a very different scene from that which would have greeted pioneering drover Joseph Hawdon and his companion Charles Bonney in 1838 when they overlanded 340 head of cattle from Hawdon's station near Albury along the Murray and across to Adelaide. Parched and no doubt weary of the sandhill country they'd crossed, Hawdon was relieved to find "a fine lake, of fresh water, about 30 miles [19 km] in circumference" and named it Lake Bonney in honour of his "friend and fellow traveller".

Though one of the youngest of the Riverland towns, Barmera, 30 km south-west of Renmark, is much loved for its lake, a popular venue for all types of water sports. The lake is tethered to the Murray by a braided network of wetlands and waterways, most notably Nockburra and Chambers creeks, and the picturesque Loch Luna Game Reserve, just 6 km to the east of the river. This was our next destination.

Waking to my first sunrise at Loch Luna Eco-stay, a low-key but comfortable lodge in the reserve, I was treated to a magical light show. The soft pink of dawn spread across the peaceful wetlands, accentuating the ruby-red azolla fern that shimmered on the current. For several quiet moments the sky blushed. The waterfowl were just beginning to stir in their roosts when the sun fiercely glared over the horizon. With that, the muted dawn hues floated off on the brightening sky.

After breakfast I chatted with Eco-stay's owners and the unofficial custodians of the wetlands, Carol and Chris Ball. On top of catering to visitors with an interest in the spectacular natural surrounds, they tend 10 ha of wine grapes.

"Loch Luna is on the Murray floodplain, and when Lock 3 was installed in 1925, 2 km to the west, it flooded the floodplain and this became a permanent wetland," Carol explained.

Plump grapefruit are now only a small part of the harvest on the 40 ha property Effie Vrastaminos and her family run at Berri, in the SA Riverland. Traditional crops such as citrus and stone fruits are slowly being replaced by wine grapes to fulfill the Greek family's contractual obligations to nearby Berri Estates, the largest winery and distillery in the Southern Hemisphere. Supply contracts with 850 independent growers give the winery more than 100,000 tonnes of grapes – about half the total quantity grown in the Riverland – to crush for at least 75 million litres of wine a year.

Cool comfort. From left, Claire, Luke, Katie and Mark Lohmeyer make a splash at the Renmark Public Pool (above), while a jetskier skims the Murray's spangled surface (above right) at Walker Flat, between Mannum and Swan Reach. Soaring summer temperatures send many people racing for the Murray's refreshing waters, an adventure playground spanning 642 km in SA.

"It is reputedly the largest wetland on the Murray in SA. It's a drought refuge for waterfowl and a resting place for migratory birds. The drowned river red gums provide important breeding habitat for birds like the darter and the white-bellied sea-eagle."

The Loch Luna Game Reserve game reserve was declared in 1985 to protect 1905 ha of what was deemed significant bird habitat. It is one of the few places on the Murray where sea-eagles are known to breed, usually during August and September, and a further 250 bird species have been recorded in the region. From a hillside overlooking the vineyard and wetlands, Carol and I watched a lone canoeist manoeuvre between red gum skeletons just beyond the lake's lignum-laced shoreline. Paddlers on the Chambers Creek and Nockburra Creek canoe reaches often see sacred kingfishers, regent parrots, white-plumed honeyeaters, coots and little pied cormorants, variegated fairy-wrens and dusky moorhens or hear the melodic song of the clamorous reed-warbler. "We pride ourselves in offering our guests peace and tranquillity," Carol said.

The visitors to the Overland Corner Hotel, 4 km to the north-west on the Old Coach Road, were a far more rambunctious crowd in its early days of operation than they are today. The hotel was built in 1859 of locally quarried limestone, red gum and native pine, and its main clients were riverboat crews, Cobb & Co. coach passengers and the tireless drovers who rested their stock here while working the "long paddock" between NSW and Adelaide.

Denizens of the Pelican Point Nudist Resort lay bare their inhibitions while taking the waters of Lake Bonney, near Barmera. Anyone from priests and professors to Japanese tourists frequents this free-spirited lakefront holiday destination, which abuts a designated nudist beach. "We respect other people's right to wear clothes but here they're not optional," said co-owner Rex Bakes.

The opalescent wetlands (right) of Nockburra Creek and Loch Luna Game Reserve braid the floodplain between Cobdogla and Kingston-on-Murray. About 1100 wetlands fringe the Murray Valley in semi-arid SA, two of which are recognised under the Ramsar Convention as being of international importance. Although the number of species has fallen in such wetlands as a result of less frequent flooding, the floodplain waters still contain many more species than the river channel itself. Seventy-five per cent of the 13,287 ha Murray River NP is floodplain, to the delight of these Australian shelducks (below) at Katarapko Creek, near Loxton. They typically rest on the water's edge by day and feed on plants in the shallow waters in the afternoon. Another of Katarapko Creek's residents is the yellow-billed spoonbill (opposite), which probes the same shallow waters for insects, crustaceans, fish and molluscs. Birds are the most conspicuous of the Murray River's resident wildlife, capitalising on the variety of riverine, grassland, wetland and woodland habitats.

Although Overland Corner is no more than a handful of houses today, it must have been a crowded corner in the 1870s, when sometimes as many as 30,000 sheep and several mobs of cattle would overnight on the common.

Entering the cool interior of the pub on a balmy summer night 130 years later I was surprised at how many drinkers breasted the bar. The rustic floor is of red gum parquetry, and the hotel's builders, brothers William, Henry and George Brand, are captured in a ghostly portrait that hangs from the wall. Legend has it that bushranger Captain Moonlite (alias Andrew Scott) frequented the hotel in 1879 while on the run from the NSW and Victorian constabulary. He is said to have drunk inside the pub while still on his horse, insisting that both the front and rear doors be kept open in case he needed to make a hasty getaway.

"The hotel has an interesting past," said Chris Nash, one of four licensees approved by the pub's owner, the National Trust of SA. "The laundry used to be a morgue – they took the doors off to make coffins – and the museum was the post office; it still has the original postmaster's desk. Everyone who comes through has a ghost story to tell about the place."

The ghosts of lesser-known Overland Corner residents are locked within the steep limestone cliffs that shepherd the Murray here. The rock that forms the cliffs consists almost entirely of fossils, and some of them – ornate corals, shellfish and the occasional shark's tooth – date back 15 million years to a time when the area was covered by a warm sea. There are even reports of a seal being spotted at Overland Corner as recently as 1890. It could never happen today; the salt water of the Southern Ocean is firmly locked out by barrages at Goolwa, near the Murray's mouth, and the only salt intrusions into the river these days – and they are considerable – are those that occur naturally or have been generated by poor irrigation and farming methods.

About 75 km west of Overland Corner we paused in out travels to visit the Nor' West Bend Living Museum. We'd been warned not to be late to this little-known museum. Viewings of the eccentric collection are by appointment only and its curator, 94-year-old Albert Brockmeyer, is a stickler for punctuality. Knowing this, Bill and I arrived early. Turning into Albert's dirt driveway, we found him at the woodheap, hard at work with an axe.

A confirmed bachelor, with milky blue eyes, Albert told me he bought Nor' West Bend station, originally covering 5180 sq. km, in 1936. By the look of his yard, he hasn't discarded a single skerrick of its contents since.

"Back in 1856 the station used to stretch from here to the NSW border and employ well over 100 staff," he said. "It was one of the first properties settled in the district and used to run 60,000 sheep and cattle and 200 horses. The early owners made their fortunes here. The wool was sent bale by bale down to the river's edge by flying fox, then it went to Goolwa by paddle-steamer and on to Adelaide and England. Today the property is just 3000 acres [1215 ha]. We run 1000 sheep, mostly on the river flats."

Ushering us into the shade of the homestead, Albert opened the door of the old schoolroom-cum-station store, now chock-a-block with collectables and peculiar mementoes of times

Skippy the kangaroo completes an authentic country scene at the Loxton Historical Village, which traces the region's development from the clearing of mallee scrub to early fruit-growing and irrigation. An eclectic collection of 30 period-furnished buildings and exhibits, including an aptly named rib-breaker plough and a vintage saddlery, celebrates the bush ingenuity and determination of the Riverland pioneers.

long past. Until it was closed in 1878 and converted into a store, the one-room school instilled learning and discipline in kids from properties near and far. On the crowded shelves I glimpsed vials of Dr Williams's Pink Pills for Pale People, Bunyip soap packets, odd kitchen utensils, an assortment of padlocks and irons, decorative tea sets, horse bits, whips, cordial bottles still bright with their coloured waters, biscuit tins, old cameras, a pith helmet and every conceivable pharmaceutical. Spiders had decorated the darkened corners with their delicate lacework, and the scent of old brown paper hung in the air.

"I've tried to keep the museum as a living museum, not all spit and polished," said Albert, by way of explanation. "I leave everything original. I haven't dusted for years; it would ruin the atmosphere of the place."

So authentic is the schoolteacher's private room next-door that I fancied she'd only just walked across the linoleum floor. Stylish old dresses and lavish hats hung from the walls beside a simple wrought-iron bed strewn with photograph albums, and a glorious gramophone sat waiting to whirr into action on a writing desk.

The collection outside was every bit as impressive. Dotted about the yard and tucked away in several old sheds were all manner of contraptions: scarifiers, wagons, steam engines, tractors, old saddlery and leather goods, a beautifully kept hawker's wagon and countless more devices that had all been useful in the past.

Memories are as thick as the cobwebs in the Nor' West Bend Living Museum, near Morgan. Until he died recently, this former sheep property was curated by Albert Brockmeyer (above left), pictured in the old station store. The station once covered 5180 sq. km and employed more than 100 staff. It was considerably bigger than the Murray River Camel Farm upstream, where raconteur and adventurer Rex Ellis and his well-balanced companion Stubby (above) treat guests to riverfront camel rides.

A SALTY LEGACY

From 1829 to 1830 explorer Charles Sturt became probably the first person to document the presence of salt in the Murray–Darling system.

Salt occurs naturally in the river and comes from the surrounding rocks and soils of the Murray Valley. Some of this salt was deposited over the past 65 million years, when the land was periodically inundated by vast inland seas.

Though weathering of these rocks and soils releases some of the remaining salt they contain, the main source of salt in the river system is that which accumulates in the groundwater from rainfall, which contains low concentrations of salt.

Under natural conditions, the salt stored in the groundwater did little harm. But human activities that have caused watertables to rise, such as irrigation and large-scale tree clearing for agriculture, have mobilised the great quantities of salt previously locked underground. Today these activities contribute some 60 per cent of the salt entering the Murray River.

Especially in the mid- and lower Murray, weirs and some lake storages have also created the mechanism for more salt to be added to the system. In creating a new river height upstream, these structures have forced salty groundwater to rise downstream and enter the river. Additionally, regulation of and diversions from the river have reduced river flow, thereby reducing dilution.

Dryland salinity is caused mostly by the replacement of deep-rooted native vegetation with shallow-rooted agricultural crops. Native plants absorb much of the rain that falls and take up moisture from the soil like a wick, releasing it through their leaves in a process called transpiration. If the plants are removed and replaced by shallow-rooted crops, rain seeps deep into the soil, raising the level of groundwater that may already be moderately salty.

As the groundwater rises, it passes through layers of salt deposited prehistorically, dissolves it and becomes even more salty. Within 2 m of the soil surface, this salt-laden water can poison most vegetation. When it reaches the surface it forms a crystalline crust.

Irrigation water penetrating the soil acts in the same way as rainfall. If the watertable is above the river level, the water draining from irrigated paddocks carries the extra salt into the river.

Salinity concentration is exacerbated in the arid and semi-arid regions of the lower Murray, where the river flows slower and the ground water holds naturally high concentrations of salt. Evaporation increases in this hot country, concentrating the salt left behind in the river.

One way of combating the Murray's increasing salinisation is to intercept saline groundwater before it reaches the river and pump it from deep bores to disposal areas such as the Stockyard Plain Disposal Basin Reserve, 15 km south-west of Waikerie. About 105 tonnes of salt a day enters the river along a 20 km stretch near the town.

By the time I'd surveyed the full collection, the sun was beating down with a vengeance and we were relieved to seek out the shade – and Albert – to bid our goodbyes. Just 250 mm of rain falls in the Riverland annually, and it has a reputation for sizzling summers. It's not the climate for me, I told Albert. "I like the warm weather," he replied, returning to chop wood. "When it's a hundred [38° F] I'm at my best."

Like those of most Murray communities, the members of Morgan's 400-strong population who don't already live on the river can generally be found beside it during hot weather. In need of a refreshing dip after leaving Albert and travelling the 5 km into the town, Bill and I joined some of the folk splashing about on its banks. At Morgan the Murray escapes from its gorge and makes a sharp left-hand turn to begin its final southward leg to the sea. And it's here that our dry continent's dependence on its life-giving artery is best illustrated.

Approaching Morgan from the north-east, I'd seen a pair of massive concrete pipes spearing off across the arid plains. They extend 360 km and supply water to Whyalla, a city of more than 25,000 souls near the head of Spencer Gulf. One pipe was built in 1940–44 as part of the war effort and the second added in the 1960s to meet the growing urban and industrial needs for treated water in the northern parts of the State.

Houseboats are as thick as ducks on the Murray in SA, where expansive reaches alternate with sandy beaches, and the tiny town of Swan Reach is a popular stopover point for free-wheeling families (above left). Motorists need to plan their crossings carefully, as only five bridges span the Murray in this State. The Morgan ferry (above) is one of 12 that operate 24 hours a day free of charge.

A patchwork of irrigated crops is nourished by the Murray at Lyrup, near Berri, in the SA Riverland. Lyrup was one of 11 irrigation-based communal villages that the SA Government founded on the river in the late 1800s. By 1900 the experiment had failed and Lyrup was the only settlement not amalgamated into private or government irrigation schemes.

Further downstream, a pipeline at Swan Reach shoots water to the Yorke Peninsula, another at Mannum slakes Adelaide's thirst directly through the metropolitan reticulation system, and still others at Murray Bridge and Tailem Bend channel water to the Onkaparinga River (near Hahndorf) and Keith, in the State's far south-east. Without the Murray, the growth and economic development of industry and agriculture in significant parts of SA would have been severely limited.

"Up to 90 per cent of all South Australians receive some Murray River water," said Philip Pfeiffer, Murray–Darling Basin Commission liaison officer for the SA Water Corporation. "In an average year, the Murray satisfies half metropolitan Adelaide's domestic and industrial water needs; in a dry year that can rise to 85 per cent."

Morgan's fate has always been inextricably linked with water. While houseboats and power-boats now bob like ducks on this reach of the Murray, Morgan was once more accustomed to paddleboat parades. The town's growth mirrored that of the river trade and received an enormous boost in 1878, when the railway arrived from Adelaide. Morgan soon became a port for Darling and upper-Murray steamers eager for a fast connection with Adelaide. Its wharf hummed with the comings and goings of gangs of industrious men working continuous shifts to unload cargoes of wool, grain, timber, dried fruit and dairy produce.

A massive red gum timber wharf 60 m long is all that remains today of the structure that once stretched for 168 m. The adjoining railway station has fared better, even though the line closed in 1969, ending a turbulent 91 years of railway history. The station master's residence is in mint condition and privately occupied and the old railway office and rest rooms have been transformed into the quaint Port of Morgan's Historic Museum. On the tranquil morning that I visited, I found it hard to picture the heady days when this was the second busiest port in SA, long queues of laden steamers and barges stretched downstream from the wharf waiting their turn to unload and six trains were dispatched daily to Port Adelaide. But inside the museum the glory days are well remembered.

Sandwiched between the corrugated-iron walls, charts and riverboat memorabilia compete for attention with flags and strange, salvaged items. My guide, museum curator John Seton, described the frantic scene during the port's heyday in the 1860s. "They burnt wood 24 hours a day to operate the five steam-powered cranes that unloaded paddle-steamers along the wharf," he said. "It was the railway that made this town, providing a link with the coastal port of Adelaide, but it was also the growth of the railway that virtually killed this town, bringing to an end the riverboat era."

Steaming back in time

The flap, flap, flap of paddlewheel blades heralded the approach of the grand lady of the Murray River long before she came into view around the bend, all 1700 tonnes and three radiant decks of her. Adorned with maroon ironwork, twin funnels and a 14-tonne stern paddlewheel, the *Murray Princess* was more Mississippi than Murray, but for sheer size and originality she was hard to surpass. That's why Bill and I had jumped at the chance to enjoy an overnight passage on the largest vessel operating on the river as it surged from Swan Reach, 70 km south of Morgan, upstream to Blanchetown.

The ship's personable cruise director, Ian Werfel, showed us to our cabins, gave us a safety demonstration and then escorted us to the bridge. In this spacious control room we met first mate Terry Salmond, who was sweating through his second day at the helm. If cool captain Tony Smith, a veteran of nine years on the *Murray Princess*, was nervous about Terry's performance, he wasn't showing it. Drawing on extensive experience of the Murray's complex channel, he patiently guided Terry from one side of the wide river to the next.

"To get to be captain, you have to know where you are on any stretch of the river," softly spoken Tony said. "You've got to know exactly when to swap sides and what's underneath you. With a draught of 1.1 m, we touch the bottom at times."

As we glided past cliffs lacquered in gold by the setting sun, Tony agreed that it's the size and grandeur of the *Murray Princess*, conjuring up memories of the more romantic and elegant days of river travel, that attracts most passengers. Many of those delighting in this five-day cruise from Mannum to Morgan were elderly folk from Adelaide, content to lounge about on deck, read, play cards and board games, or take in the passing vistas. Dining and entertainment are finely orchestrated each evening, and Ian attends to almost their every need.

"We get a lot of return passengers," Tony said. "One lady from Port Pirie has done 80 cruises; she did her 78th on her 78th birthday."

As the sun melted into the horizon, Terry steadied and moored the 67 m long *Murray Princess* in a stiff southerly wind – no easy feat – beside the Murray's junction with Moorundie Creek, on Portee station, mid-way between Swan Reach and Blanchetown. Once extra lines had been secured aft and Terry had retired to wring out his shirt and order a beer, Tony also relaxed and showed me some of his artwork – intricate ink sketches of red gums, possums and river scenes inspired by his travels.

"There's still so much of the river I haven't seen," he said ruefully. "I've always wanted to have something smaller and go all the way up the Murray and its tributaries."

The following morning, Australia Day, dawned cool and breezy, but the welcome was warm at Blanchetown, where a crowd had assembled to watch Tony guide the 15 m wide vessel into the chamber of the lock, the first built on the Murray, in 1922. It was a cosy fit, with just 1 m to spare on each side, and the spectators applauded his dexterity. Waving Australian flags, the crew then farewelled Bill and me as we left the *Murray Princess* to catch a lift back to our vehicle at Swan Reach.

All along the Murray, families were revelling in the fine conditions. At Walker Flat, south of Swan Reach, we paused to take in the spectacle. Squinting against the dazzle of the foil-bright surface, I watched jetskiers, rowers and powerboats tracking across the Murray's waters.

There was no escaping the river-based recreation at Mannum either. Holidaymakers packed the riverfront reserves there and cruise boats overflowed with passengers. Rather than

Ralph Bowden, SA Water's senior country turncock, inspects the 360 km Morgan–Whyalla pipeline, which delivers Murray water to Port Augusta and Whyalla. It was the first of several pipelines built to supply half of SA's domestic and industrial water from the river in an average year and up to 90 per cent during a dry year.

fall in with the majority, I was keen to board the paddle-steamer *Marion*, a 102-year-old vessel painstakingly restored by Mannum Dock Museum Board volunteers. Arthur Baum and wife Marie, the board's chairperson, showed me around the handsome boat, possibly the world's only remaining original wood-fired passenger steamer with overnight accommodation.

Mannum is a fitting home for a lady of such pedigree. William Randell launched the *Mary Ann* in 1853 just 5 km upstream from there, opening one of the most spirited chapters in Australian history. Marie said the *Marion* began life as a barge in 1896 and served as a floating store before being refitted to carry cargo and passengers. It was one of the first steamers to run passenger cruises for the Murray Shipping Company and plied regularly between Morgan and Mildura before ending up as a boarding house at Berri. "She's had a very chequered history," Marie said.

After the National Trust bought the vessel and put it into dry dock at Mannum. It was then sold to the Mannum District Council, who took responsibility for its restoration and conservation. In what Marie describes as a "labour of love", volunteers toiled for more than 150,000 hours over the next 10 years to restore the vessel. In the narrow captain's cabin, I found the intimate personal objects the most fascinating: a cut-throat razor, a worn brush-and-comb set, spectacles, and an alarm clock that undoubtedly was used to rouse the crew on many an early morning.

"Paddleboats have played an important role in the lives of river people because so many worked on the boats at one time or another," Marie said as we looked in on the stylish, timber-lined dining room. "We meet such lovely people who have had an association with the *Marion* and it's wonderful to hear their stories."

In the wheelhouse I had the good fortune to meet Michelle Trellean, whose grandfather, Percy, worked on the *Marion* for a time on the Murrumbidgee River. Her six-year-old daughter, Danika, hanging like a monkey from the large wheel, seemed determined to follow in her great-grandfather's footsteps.

Mannum to the sea

South of Mannum the Murray's leisurely passage to the Southern Ocean takes it through the lush dairy pastures around Murray Bridge. Most of the region's milk is now transported by gleaming road tankers to the town's factory, but in the early 1900s a charming fleet of little milk boats collected it. Many people made a living directly from the Murray in those days, while others made it their home, earning the tag "river rats".

It's a nickname Paul and Zaiga Abend have been proud to bear during 14 years on the Murray aboard *Last Resort*. When Bill and I found them docked at the Wellington Marina, near where the Murray spills into Lake Alexandrina, they'd settled in for a few months to avoid the "noisy ones" that visit the Murray in summer.

"We don't have a schedule; we're retired and we can please ourselves," said Paul, a crusty skipper, as we shared morning tea on their home's sunny deck. "You can cast off and

Dwarfed by the PS *Murray Princess* (above), the largest boat operating on the river, school mates take a break from waterskiing on Australia Day. After docking here for the night, midway between Swan Reach and Blanchetown, the 1700-tonne grand dame continued north through the Murray Gorge (opposite) on its five-night passage from Mannum to Morgan.

Pelicans feed frenziedly on bony bream (above) stunned during their exit from the Blanchetown lock spillway while human anglers try their luck for carp upstream of the lock (above right). Lock 1 at Blanchetown was the first of six locks and weirs built across the Murray in SA to ease navigation, help in the diversion of water for irrigation and improve river regulation.

move home whenever you want. Sometimes the biggest question of the day is whether to use worms or shrimps for fishing bait!"

The couple last lived on land at Victor Harbor in 1985, but they don't appear to want for anything in their well-equipped, 20 m floating home. With a sitting room, library, kitchen, bathroom and three guest rooms, as well as their own master bedroom, they have ample space to "lose each other", as Zaiga says. All this and two television sets, an organ and even a chandelier for those special occasions. They must keep an eye on the river level and river obstacles and carefully plan their sewage pump-outs and shopping expeditions, but these are minor adjustments, amply compensated for by the swag of friends they've made along the Murray. "You can't sneak past some riverfront properties without calling in," said Zaiga. "Quite often there are signs on the bank stating: '*Last Resort* pull in here'."

It's an unorthodox lifestyle but one that Paul, 60, and Zaiga, 57, are quick to defend. "Some people think it is unstructured but it's just that our village is long and skinny," Paul said. "The Murray River is one of the last free bits of country around. The river is our home; we see ourselves as caretakers of it for life." Again I was reminded of Ratty's views about his river in *Wind in the Willows*: "It's brother and sister to me, and aunts, and company, and food and drink, and (naturally) washing. It's my world, and I don't want any other. What it hasn't got is not worth having, and what it doesn't know is not worth knowing."

Cliffs shepherd the khaki Murray through the settlement of Walker Flat, between Mannum and Swan Reach. Lake Bywater, the stretch of water beyond, is shallow and suitable only for canoeists and windsurfers, but full advantage is taken of the deep water that pools in the main river channel behind weirs for a range of sports. More than 1100 sq. km of parks and reserves protect the Murray Valley in SA. Tourism contributes about $150 million a year to the State's economy.

"We're fiercely protective of the Murray; it's our neighbourhood," said river gypsy Paul Abend (above), pictured with his wife, Zaiga, and dog Pug aboard their houseboat *Last Resort* at the Wellington Marina, in the river's lower SA reaches. Just south of Wellington the Murray enters Lake Alexandrina and its final passage to the sea is barred by five barrages, including the Tauwitchere Barrage (right), which prevents the lake's fresh water from mixing with the salt water of the Coorong beyond.

From Wellington I watched Lake Alexandrina swallow the broad river and eventually disgorge it through the Goolwa barrages. The Murray's final destination, the Southern Ocean, lay just beyond. The river port of Goolwa chaperones the Murray on its date with destiny. Historically one of the largest boatbuilding and repair centres on the Murray, a maritime survey centre and customs checkpoint, Goolwa is today an enchanting base for fishing, nature and boating enthusiasts. The wild Coorong, a shallow saltwater lagoon that stretches for some 140 km south-east from Murray Mouth, lies a short distance away, and myriad secluded bays and coves entice people with a sense of adventure.

Under an overcast sky I hopped aboard the *Spirit of the Coorong* for a cruise with captain Jock Veenstra to explore the Coorong's waters and the Sir Richard and Younghusband peninsulas, which guard the river's mouth. Jock spends six days a week on the water, as his father did before him, and is a keen observer of the Murray's movements. Only the year before, the river had shrunk so much that its water didn't make it past Murray Mouth to the Coorong. A sandbar appeared across the entrance to the lagoon, barring entry of both fresh water and vessels. I wasn't surprised to hear that, on average, the river disgorges into the sea only 21 per cent of the water that it did before river regulation.

"Since 1981 the mouth has shifted 1 km westwards towards Goolwa," Jock said as we skirted Hindmarsh Island. "It closed for some time in 1981, and then a passage was dug out by excavators. It requires a substantial flow of water each day to keep the mouth open."

▦ Increasing water diversion upstream, shifting sandbars and a succession of dry years have reduced the Murray to a mere trickle at its mouth, but the exit has closed only once in recorded history, in April 1981. It came within a whisker of closing again in February 2000 (left), when it assumed this deltaic appearance. The Murray's fortunes are keenly followed by the people of Goolwa, the last town on the river, where Phil and Joy Stolz (above) enjoy the privileges of a private jetty in front of their riverside home.

Having taken his vessel through the Goolwa lock, Jock pointed to the south and the distant breakers that marked the Murray's exit to the sea. "A signalman used to be based at the mouth," he said. "Now, only a few boats can venture in and out because of the sandbar, and it can be pretty treacherous. It gets down to 30 m wide and knee-deep when there's little flow coming down the river."

We approached the teal-coloured waters of the narrow river mouth. From the bow I watched a couple of fishermen wade out across it with long beach rods, casting for mullet and mulloway (jewfish) attracted by the fresh water. Beyond them, the river, brackish now, moved out past the break. And then it vanished in the infinity of ocean. After all the triumphs and travails of this iconic waterway, it seemed a modest finale.

My journey had ended with the Murray's. The only way to go now was back. I turned inland to retrace my steps.

In *The Nile of Australia: Nature's Gateway to the Interior*, David Gordon wrote in 1906: "The Australian who has not been afloat on the waters of the Murray and its many affluents does not know his native country ..."

I can't presume to say that during my 10 weeks of exploring the Murray I'd come to know everything about my native country. But I do know that I will never see it in the same light again.

Residents of the wildly beautiful southern reaches of the Murray River have much to celebrate. At Milang, on the shores of Lake Alexandrina, they gather each year on 9 February (above) to toast Charles Sturt's naming of the lake, in 1830, after Princess Alexandrina, later Queen Victoria. Sturt effectively ruled out commercial navigation of the Murray's mouth. Variations in river flow, unpredictable ocean currents and strong winds make it hazardous, but with the mulloway (jewfish) running, there was no stopping this pair of fishermen (opposite top). A safer pursuit is to cruise aboard the *Spirit of the Coorong* to Godfreys Landing (opposite bottom) in 47,000 ha Coorong NP, the last major feature of the Murray's epic journey from the Australian Alps to the sea.

Travel advice

Getting there and getting around

You can easily reach destinations along the Murray River by car, train or bus, or by plane to Mildura from Sydney, Canberra, Melbourne or Adelaide.

The Murray Valley Highway runs almost parallel to the river in Victoria, as do the Riverina and Sturt highways in NSW. The Sturt Highway remains the main riverside thoroughfare into SA as far as Blanchetown, where it connects with other regional routes heading south.

Albury–Wodonga is a central base for excursions to the upper Murray. It's about a 300 km drive from Melbourne on the Hume Freeway, about 600 km from Sydney on the Hume Highway and 350 km from Canberra. It's also serviced daily by regional airlines from Sydney, Melbourne and Canberra and daily XPT trains from Sydney and Melbourne.

In the central Murray, Echuca or Swan Hill are accessible departure points. Echuca is 200 km from Melbourne. Swan Hill is 340 km from Melbourne on the Calder Highway (as far as Bendigo) and the Lodden Valley Highway. Mildura is about 550 km from Melbourne on the Calder Highway. There are daily flights to Mildura from Melbourne, Sydney and Adelaide.

Renmark, centre of the Riverland, is 250 km from Adelaide on the Sturt Highway. Coaches and connections to the Riverland are available from all mainland capital cities.

Most of the Murray River valley's roads are negotiable by conventional vehicles in dry weather. However, conditions can change dramatically, especially in the mallee country. Some tracks become impassable in wet weather. If in doubt, check road conditions with authorities or national park staff before visiting.

Weather

The weather along the Murray is as varied as the terrain, so be prepared for anything. In the high country, conditions can change unexpectedly and bring storms and snowfalls. In contrast, late spring, summer and autumn temperatures in the mallee country can exceed 40°C.

Generally summer is hot and dry, with a high fire danger, and winter is cool and mild. Average summer temperatures vary between 26°C and 40°C and winter temperatures range from 10°C to 16°C.

What to take

Travellers are advised to carry broad-spectrum sunscreen, a broad-brimmed hat, good maps and a pair of binoculars to best appreciate the varied sights. During the few hot months of summer, long pants offer good protection against the sun. In winter it can be chilly and wet, so take warmer clothing.

Some of the best bushwalking tracks along the Murray are remote. Bushwalkers should carry plenty of water, food and protective clothing, a compass and topographic maps. In remoter areas such as Hattah–Kulkyne and Murray–Sunset national parks, walkers should be experienced, well prepared and self-reliant, and they should always notify family or friends of their intentions.

Murray River water

Murray water is suitable for cooking and drinking but should be treated first, either with purifying tablets or by boiling for 30 minutes.

Avoid polluting the river or its tributaries with refuse, soap or detergent. Draw water in containers for washing purposes and dispose of the waste water in a pit dug in the soil at least 30 m from the river. Use biodegradable products where you can.

■ Victoria von Bertouch and daughter Abbie lap up the fun while tubing behind a powerboat on the Murray River just north of Blanchetown in SA.

Houseboats retire for the night as the sun sets over Swan Reach, in SA. They can be hired at many Murray towns and offer unparallelled freedom to explore the river.

Houseboats

If you prefer the flexibility of deciding how far you'll travel in a day and where you'll stop for the night, a houseboat might be for you. Most have all the comforts of home and you can choose from budget to luxury and from two to twelve berths.

Houseboats are available at many towns along the Murray. For more information in Victoria and NSW, contact the visitor information centres in Echuca, Swan Hill and Mildura. In SA, the Houseboat Hirers' Association (+ 08 8395 0999) has 128 boats on the river from Renmark to Murray Bridge.

You don't need to be a seasoned mariner to take the wheel of one of these vessels but you must be over 18 and have a current boat or car licence. Most houseboat hirers give ample information on regulations and safety procedures and all boats have two-way radios but you must tie up by sundown. Houseboats are not permitted to travel after sunset.

It's usually the responsibility of the houseboat owners, not the boat hirers, to pump out wastes at waste-disposal stations located along the river.

A comprehensive booklet is available, free, from the Houseboat Hirers' Association.

Canoeing

Canoeing is a relaxing and instructive way to explore the Murray and its braided wetlands and backwaters. Conditions vary along the river, from the narrow rapids of the upper Murray to the broader and slower reaches in SA.

In its headwaters, the river is graded 3–4, so unless you're an experienced whitewater canoeist and/or rafter, you should join a group or expedition led by an expert. The lower sections of the Murray are more typically grade 1 and suitable for family canoeing, but you should always take care. Currents and depths can be unpredictable, submerged trees are an ever-present danger and unexpected releases of water can rapidly change conditions. Check local river conditions and levels before setting out.

The Murray River has signs every 2 km from the Hume Weir to SA which indicate your distance in kilometres from the end of the Murray entrance. Should you need assistance, use these signs to indicate your position – they are blue with white numbers.

Wherever you're canoeing, stay away from weirs. Outflowing water can create a vacuum on the lower side of the weir and canoeists can be pinned against the top.

Fruit-fly exclusion zones

The major horticultural regions along the Murray in south-western NSW, northern Victoria and SA are worth millions of dollars annually and are protected by the Fruit Fly Exclusion Zone (FFEZ). It is illegal to carry fruit across the FFEZ boundary, and travellers may be subject to random road checks. You may be given an on-the-spot fine if you are found carrying fresh fruit and vegetables, so eat any fresh produce or dispose of it in the signposted roadside bins or pits before entering the FFEZ.

Camping

Camping along the banks of the Murray is one of the river's simple pleasures and there are plenty of attractive camp sites and picnic areas in national parks, state parks, forests and reserves.

As large sections of the Murray are in private property, respect boundaries and never enter private land without permission. In SA, camping is allowed on the 30 m strip of Crown land on either side of the Murray but you need permission from the land- or leaseholder to reach it.

You are encouraged to camp in designated areas, where possible, in natural clearings at least 20 m from the river's edge. It's advisable not to pitch your tent under river red gums: they are prone to drop limbs without warning.

Camping fees and fire restrictions apply in most national parks and reserves along the Murray, but it's advisable to check details with local authorities.

Where fireplaces are provided, use them. In some national parks you're not allowed to gather firewood (this is to protect native habitats) and you

The Barmah Lakes Picnic Area, in Barmah State Park, near Echuca, is just one of the many pleasant picnic spots along the Murray's peaceful shores.

should buy or bring your own. Where you're allowed to gather firewood, it must be dry timber lying on the ground. If there are no fireplaces, use a portable stove or build a small fire at least 4 m from any vegetation. Remember to put the fire out completely when leaving. Note that during high fire danger periods, only portable stoves are allowed.

If there are no toilets, bury wastes 50 cm deep at least 100 m from the river. Buried litter is usually dug up by native animals, so it's best to take it out with you.

River hazards

Water conditions in the river change rapidly and the Murray contains a variety of hidden obstacles, so swimmers should be careful. The water can be cold at any time of year and the fast current hazardous. Check the water for temperature, snags and depth before entering, avoid diving into the river and never swim near submerged or floating logs.

Currents, snags and powerboats make swimming across the river dangerous. Don't trust sandbars: they can move without warning when the water level changes and they often drop off suddenly into very deep water. The sweeping bends of a sandbar can create currents, so it's best to swim upstream well away from them.

Look out for snakes crossing the river and around riverbanks. Tiger, brown, copper and red-bellied black snakes are the most common venomous species along the Murray, but they are all protected and pose little threat if you give them a wide berth.

Fishing regulations

All the waters of the Murray River flowing downstream to the South Australian border are covered by NSW Fisheries laws, except for parts of lakes Mulwala and Hume. In Lake Mulwala and Lake Hume, the border between NSW and Victoria is the southern bank of the original Murray River course that lies under the impounded water. The waters south of this border are under the jurisdiction of the Victorian Department of Natural Resources & Environment. Tourist information is available at both of these dams and fishing information and maps to indicate the boundary are also available. Please check with the local Fisheries Office for further details if necessary.

Anglers who are 18 years and over (except holders of Commonwealth Pensioner Concession cards and Aboriginal people) must possess a Recreational Freshwater Fishing Licence to fish in non-tidal freshwaters of NSW. Licences are available from most tackle stores or by phoning 1300 369 365. For additional information about fishing on the Murray, contact NSW Fisheries on 02 9566 7888.

Anglers must possess a Victorian recreational fishing licence if fishing the Murray's southern tributaries. For information, contact Fisheries Victoria on 03 5226 4667. You don't need a licence to fish the Murray in SA; however, restrictions apply to some species. Phone Primary Industries and Resources, SA, on 08 8226 2311 for more information.

Restrictions on the fishing equipment that can be used, minimum catch lengths, bag limits, protected species and closed seasons for the Murray are described in brochures produced by each of the above State government authorities.

A closed season for Murray cod applies for the Murray from 1 September to 30 November inclusive (also applicable throughout NSW), and it is recommended that if any undesirable species, such as carp and redfin are caught they should not be returned to the water alive. Fishing closures usually exist upstream and downstream of weirs and dam wall structures and these are usually indicated by signage – if not, check with your local Fisheries Office. Anglers may use two attended lines on any impoundments, and in rivers one attended and four set lines are permitted. No set lines are allowed on the Murray River at any time between Yarrawonga Weir and Tocumwal Road bridge. This area is special because it is one of the few remaining areas that contains a wild population of trout cod, a totally protected species.

Upstream from the road bridge at Tintaldra, all the waters of the Murray within NSW are notified trout waters and the trout regulations apply. No set lines are permitted but you may use one rod in the river or two rods in the impoundment.

Boating and skiing

NSW and SA boating regulations apply along the Murray River. All boat operators must be licensed

■ Time marches slowly for fishermen at Blanchetown, SA. No licence is required to fish the Murray in this State but restrictions apply.

and must carry the minimum safety equipment as required by regulation. The operator must obey all boating rules, observe all signs and buoys, and be wary of swimmers at all times. It is recommended that a copy of the *New South Wales Safe Boating Handbook* and the *South Australian Recreational Boating Safety Handbook* be obtained. For more information, phone the NSW Waterways Authority information line on 02 9563 8555 or its regional offices at Albury (02 6021 7188), Moama (03 5482 1300) or Mildura (03 5023 4610). The marine safety division of the Marine Operations Group Transport SA can be contacted on 08 8347 5001.

Give other boats on the river a wide berth and apply at all times the simple rule of the river: keep to the right. A vessel to your starboard, or right-hand side, always has right of way, similar to motor vehicles at a roundabout. Boats should be launched only from designated boat ramps as river banks are prone to damage and erosion.

Reduce your boat's speed to 4 knots within 100 m of a ferry crossing. When approaching a crossing, warn the ferry driver when not more than 800 m and not less than 400 m away, with a prolonged (approximately 4–6 seconds) whistle or horn blast and proceed carefully. If the ferry is crossing, wait until the way is clear and the ferry operator has given the all-clear signal. Some ferry cables lie just under the water's surface and need to be lowered to allow a boat through.

When nearing a lock, either sound three long blasts (approximately 4–6 seconds duration) on a horn or siren, wave a flag or flash a light. When 150 m from the lock wait for the lockmaster's permission to proceed, usually indicated by a green flag or a fixed or flashing green light. When entering the lock follow the signs and the lockmaster's instructions, and line your boat up straight to enter the lock chamber.

Skiing is not advisable where the banks are steep or where there are known snags. Watch for "No Ski" and "No Wash" signs. Lifejackets, one for each person, should be carried aboard all craft. You must obey the relevant State rules when waterskiing. In SA, a 4 knot (7km/h) speed limit applies when within 50 m of a person in the water, a vessel or buoy displaying a "diver below" flag, a person in or on a canoe, kayak, sailing boat or similar small, unpowered recreational vessel. Remember that 0.05 "Drink Driving" rules apply when boating. In the case of waterskiing for example, "Drink Driving" rules apply to driver, skier and observer.

The best guides for anyone exploring the Murray by boat are the *Murray River Pilot*, by Ronald and Margaret Baker and William Reschke. Available by phoning 08 8555 1359 or 08 8270 3716, this covers the lower lakes and Coorong to the SA–NSW border. *River Murray Charts* by Maureen Wright (available by phoning 08 8892 2461) covers the river from

The 1838 Morphett's Ferry, superseded by the Wellington ferry, became the first means of crossing the Murray in SA.

Renmark to Yarrawonga. Both are indispensable, practical guides to every bend in the river and list the contact numbers of ferry and bridge operators and lockmasters (to arrange passages through locks).

If travelling by boat along the Murray to Goolwa, you might like to record your trip in the National Register at Signal Point by phoning 08 8555 3488.

Vehicular Ferries

Vehicular ferries are to be found along the Murray River where there are no bridge crossings.

Most punts have diesel motors that drag them along steel cables strung from bank to bank.

Bridges are reasonably well spaced along the Murray but in remoter areas vehicular ferries may be your only option, so plan your river crossings carefully. Some ferries operate 24 hours a day while others are limited to set hours, so check the times and load limits locally.

TOURIST INFORMATION CENTRES AND NATIONAL PARKS

Tourism Murray River
PO Box 717
Albury, NSW 2640
Ph: 1800 508 867
Fax: 02 6040 1360

Upper Murray Tourism
PO Box 55
Tallangatta, Victoria 3700
Ph: 02 6076 9009
Email: veronicab@towong.vic.gov.au

Albury Wodonga Visitor Information Centre and Booking Service
Gateway Island
Lincoln Causeway
Wodonga, Victoria 3690
Ph: 1800 800 743 or 02 6041 3875
Fax: 02 6021 0322
Email: info@cow.mav.asn.au

Corowa Information Centre
88 Sanger Street
Corowa, NSW 2646
Ph: 1800 814 054 or 02 6033 3221
Fax: 02 6033 3587
Email: corowa.tourinfo@albury.net.au

Yarrawonga-Mulwala Visitor Information Centre
1 Irvine Parade
Yarrawonga, Victoria 3730
Ph: 1800 062 260 or 03 5744 1989
Fax: 03 5744 3149
Email: moirato@cnl.com.au

Cobram-Barooga Visitor Information Centre
Corner Station Street and Punt Road
Cobram, Victoria 3644
Ph: 1800 607 607 or 03 5872 2132
Fax: 03 5871 1727
Email: cbt@cnl.com.au

Tocumwal Visitor Information Centre
Foreshore Park
Tocumwal, NSW 2714
Ph: 03 5874 2131 or 1800 677 271
Fax: 03 5874 3300
Email: tocinfo@cnl.com.au

Echuca-Moama Visitor Information Centre
2 Heygarth Street
Echuca, Victoria 3564
Ph: 03 5480 7555 or 1800 804 446
Fax: 03 5482 6413
Email: mbenett@river.net.au
Website: www.echucamoama.com.au

Golden Rivers Country Visitor Information Centre
25 Murray Street
Barham, NSW 2732
Ph: 03 5453 3100 or 1800 621 882
Fax: 03 5453 3122
email: goldrivr@swanhill.net.au
Website: www.goldenrivers.com

Swan Hill Development and Information Centre
306 Campbell Street
Swan Hill, Victoria 3585
Ph: 1800 625 373 or 03 5032 3033
Fax: 03 5032 3032
Email: tourism@swanhill.vic.gov.au
Website: murrayoutback.org.au

Mildura Visitor Information Centre
180-190 Deakin Avenue
Mildura, Victoria 3500
Ph: 1800 039 043 or 03 5021 4424
Fax: 03 5021 1836
Email: tourism@mildura.vic.gov.au
Website: www.murrayoutback.org.au

Renmark Paringa Visitor Information Centre
Murray Avenue
Renmark, South Australia 5341
Ph: 08 8586 6704
Fax: 08 8586 5444
Email: tourist@riverland.net.au

Berri Tourist and Travel Centre
24 Vaughan Terrace
Berri, South Australia 5343
Ph: 08 8582 1655
Fax: 08 8582 3201

Loxton Tourism and Art Centre
Bookpurnong Terrace
Loxton, South Australia 5333
Ph: 08 8584 7919
Fax: 08 8584 6225

Barmera Travel Centre
Barwell Avenue
Barmera, South Australia 5345
Ph: 08 8588 2289
Fax: 08 8588 2777
Email: brmtrvl@sa.ozland.net.au

Mannum Tourist Information Centre
Arnold Park
Randell Street
Mannum, South Australia 5238
Ph: 08 8569 1303
Fax: 08 8569 2733

Murray Bridge Information and Tourist Centre
3 South Terrace
Murray Bridge, South Australia 5253
Ph: 08 8532 6660 or 08 8532 2900
Fax: 08 8532 5288
Email: g.braendler@rcmb.sa.gov.au

Tailem Bend Tourist Information Centre
Railway Terrace
Tailem Bend, South Australia 5260
Ph/Fax: 08 8572 4277

Melaleuca Tourist Information Centre
76 Princes Highway
Meningie, South Australia 5264
Ph/Fax: 08 8575 1259

Signal Point Visitor Information Centre
The Wharf
Goolwa, South Australia 5214
Ph: 08 8555 3488
Fax: 08 8555 3810

National Parks

Burrowa Pine Mountain National Park
☎ 02 6076 1655

Barmah State Park
☎ 03 5866 2702

Hattah-Kulkyne National Park
☎ 03 5029 3259

Murray Sunset National Park
☎ 03 5028 1260

Murray River National Park
Murraylands Regional Office
SA NPWS
☎ 08 8595 2111

Coorong National Park
☎ 08 8575 1200.

TRAVEL DIRECTORY

Transportation

Coach companies
The **Premier Stateliner Coach Group** (☎ 8415 5555 in Adelaide or 8586 6468 in Renmark) operates services from Adelaide to: Renmark, Berri, Glossop, Barmera, Cobdogla, Loxton, Moorook, Waikerie, Blanchetown and Goolwa.

Greyhound Pioneer (☎ 13 20 30) operates from Sydney to Adelaide daily, stopping at: Renmark, Berri, Barmera, Kingston-on-Murray, Waikerie and Blanchetown. A service from Melbourne to Adelaide stops daily at Tailem Bend and Murray Bridge.

McCafferty's (☎ 8586 5965 or 13 14 99) operates from Sydney to Adelaide daily, stopping at: Renmark, Berri, Barmera, Waikerie and Blanchetown. Its service from Melbourne to Adelaide stops daily at Tailem Bend and Murray Bridge.

Train travel
The **Overland** (☎ 13 21 47) operates between Adelaide and Melbourne via Murray Bridge.

Vehicle hire
Avis (☎ 1800 225 533) and **Hertz** (☎ 13 30 39) offer vehicle rental from Adelaide or Mildura airports, with drop-offs at Mildura or Adelaide.

Caseys Limousine and Hire Cars in Waikerie (☎ 8541 3044) have chauffeur-driven cars and limousines (up to eight people) and can transport people travelling in houseboats or on tours to river towns upstream.

Murray Bridge Taxi Service and Car Hire (☎ 8531 0555) have one car and one 11-seater bus for hire, which must be returned to Murray Bridge. Advance bookings are recommended.

Key Bushwalks

The 4 km **Wetland Walking Trail** begins just west of the Port of Murthoo Customs House and proceeds along the floodplain within Chowilla Regional Reserve, 27 km north-east of Paringa.

A series of walks of varying duration (5 minutes to 2 hours) explore the riverine environment of **Paringa Paddock** between Paringa and Renmark.

Allow a few hours to enjoy the 8 km **Overland Corner Walking Trail** that loops from the Overland Corner Hotel past numerous historic and ecological sites to the Murray River and back.

Key Tourist Drives

The **Old Coach Road Vehicle Trail** is a 20 km track that highlights historic and ecological sites along the Chowilla floodplain, now part of the Bookmark Biosphere Reserve, north-east of Renmark.

A 10 km nature drive winds through the mallee of **Brookfield Conservation Park**, west of Blanchetown.

The 18 km drive along the Murray's eastern bank between Purnong and Mannum is one of the most scenic.

Canoeing Trails

There are options for one-, two- and three-day trips on the secluded waters of the **Chowilla Regional Reserve**.

The **Pike River system** south and east of Lyrup Flats (Murray River National Park) offers fine paddling on three interconnecting waterways – the Pike River, Mundic and Tanyaca creeks.

Allow 1–2 hours to complete the **Chambers Creek Canoe Trail** between Lake Bonney and the Murray River, west of Cobdogla.

A 2–3-hour paddle on the **Nockburra Creek Canoe Trail**, also provides access to the waters of the tranquil Loch Luna Game Reserve.

Tour Operators

Paringa/Renmark
Renmark River Cruises – 2-hour scenic cruises aboard the MV *River Rambler*. ☎ 8595 1862.

Barmera/Cobdogla
Riverland Leisure Canoe Tours, Barmera – 1- and 2-day Riverland canoeing tours, focusing on birdlife. ☎ 8588 2053.

Waikerie
Benson Park weekend adventure trail rides – also twilight rides, bushwalking and hay rides. ☎ 8541 2283.

Morgan
Morgan Eco-Experiences – nature walks and birdwatching tours of 1-3 hours in either floodplain or semi-arid environments. ☎ 8540 4035 or 0407 727 109.

Blanchetown/Swan Reach/Nildottie
Ngaut Ngaut Conservation Park – tour of the ancient rock shelters once occupied by the Nganguraku and Ngaiwong people. ☎ 8570 1202.

Mannum
Dragon Fly River Cruises. Commentary on history, birdlife and geology during a half-hour return cruise from Mary Ann Reserve to Ponde. Sundays, weather permitting. ☎ 8569 2631.

The Coorong
Camp Coorong – Aboriginal cultural centre. See exhibitions of Ngarrindjeri arts, craft and history, and enjoy bushwalking and other field trips. ☎ 8575 1557.

Bookmark Biosphere Reserve
Loch Luna Ecostay – tour of 2600 ha farm with vineyards, mallee vegetation and wetlands, with opportunities for bushwalking, canoeing or mountain-biking. ☎ 8588 7210, lochluna@riverland.net.au

Canoe/Boating Hire

Rivermate Boat Hire, Renmark – dinghy, flat-bottomed punt and hydraslide hire. ☎ 8586 6928.

Riverland Canoeing Adventures, Loxton North – canoe hire and advice for canoe tourers. ☎ 8584 1494.

Riverscape Canoe Hire, Murray Bridge. ☎ 8531 0855.

Goolwa Catamaran and Sailboard Hire, Barrage Road, Goolwa. ☎ 8552 8439 or 0412 421 356.

INDEX

ACKNOWLEDGEMENTS

For their assistance with this book, Australian Geographic, Amanda Burdon and Bill Bachman thank:

Jim Bowler, Melbourne University; David Breedon, Albury Backpackers and Canoe Hire; Steve and Stavroula Caracatsanoudis, Robinvale Wines; Lindsay Chugg, Linbrae Camel Farm; Ian Connellan; Rod Coombs, Riverland Fishermans' Association; David Dadd, Coorong Nature Tours; Stefano de Pieri; Peter Disher; David Eastburn; Rex and Patti Ellis, Murray River Camel Farm; Iain Ellis, Ben Gawne, Terry Hillman, John Whittington, Murray-Darling Freshwater Research Centre; Don Escott, Ross Bodey, Sportavia Soaring Centre; Boris Everson, Rapid Descents; Ross Flanigan, MV *Paradise Queen*; Steve Gibbs, Katarapko Community Action Group; Garry Hera-Singh, Lakes and Coorong Fishers; David Hill, Lin Pope, Yookamurra Sanctuary; Bill Hogg, MV *Kookaburra*; Helen Coulson, Kevin Hutchison, Anita Hunter, Port of Echuca; Trevor Jacobs, Andy Close, Rosemary Purdie, Murray-Darling Basin Commission; Max Jones; Ian Kellett, Sunraysia Steam Preservation Society; Rod Kerr, NSW Department of Land and Water Conservation; David Leslie, State Forests of NSW; Paul Lloyd, NSW Murray Wetlands Working Group; crew of *Murray Princess*, Captain Cook Cruises; Duncan McDonald, Trevor and Linda Davis, Tom Groggin station; Greg McNally; Robert Mansell; Jim Marsh, SA Water; Doug Nicholls; Graeme Padgett, Debbie Jackson, Murray River Horse Trails; Colin Pardoe, Australian Archaeological Association; Richard Patterson, Swan Hill Pioneer Settlement; Darcy Pettit; Bryan Pierce, Keith Hand, SA Research and Development Institute; Glynis Pitts, Tyntynder Homestead; Derek Ross; Tony Sharley, Primary Industries and Resources, Murray-Darling Basin; Craig Smith, NSW NPWS; the Smithwick family, Talmalmo station; Torben Sorensen, Upper Murray Holiday Resort; MariJana Southern; Shaun Stephens, North-west Region Cultural Heritage; Peter Teasdale, Nick Walton, Andy Wise, Parks Victoria; Tom and Ellen Trevorrow, Camp Coorong; Jock Veenstra, Goolwa Cruises; Ron Vise, Snowy Mountains Holidays; Paul and Victoria von Bertouch, Roonka Riverfront Cottages; Stephen Wait, Woorlong Holiday Villas; Keith Walker, University of Adelaide; Keith Ward, Natural Resources and Environment, Victoria; Bill and Judy Wells, Ournie station.

Special thanks to:
Ron Dowler, Ronnie Beauchamp, Kate Green, Teresa Lever, Kaye Demmery, Julie Stava, Belinda Henderson-Drife, Maureen Bennett, Georgina Wheeler and Carole Reid of Tourism Murray River; Philip Engelberts of the South Australian Tourism Commission; Mark Gibbs of Murraylands Regional Tourism; Michelle Hocking of Riverland Tourism and Chris Burchett of Fleurieu Tourism.